LITERARY CRITICISM AND CULTURAL THEORY

Edited by
William E. Cain
Professor of English, Wellesley College

A ROUTLEDGE SERIES

LITERARY CRITICISM AND CULTURAL THEORY

WILLIAM E. CAIN, *General Editor*

THE FICTION OF NATIONALITY
IN AN ERA OF TRANSNATIONALISM

Nyla Ali Khan

Routledge
New York & London

Excerpts from *Among the Believers,* by V. S. Naipaul, copyright 1981 by V. S. Naipaul, used by permission of Alfred A. Knopf, a division of Random House, Inc.
Excerpts from *The Shadow Lines,* by Amitav Ghosh, reprinted by permission of the author.
Excerpts from *In Custody,* by Anita Desai, reprinted by permission of the author.
Excerpts from *The Satanic Verses,* copyright 1988 by Salman Rushdie, reprinted by permission of Knopf Canada. Excerpts from *The Satanic Verses,* published by Jonathan Cape, reprinted by permission of The Random House Group Limited. Excerpts from *The Satanic Verses* used by permission of Viking Penguin, a division of Penguin Group (USA) Inc.
A version of Chapter 3 originally appeared in the *Journal of South Asian Literature,* and is reprinted here by kind permission of Surjeet Dulai.
A version of Chapter 5 originally appeared in the *Atlantic Literary Review,* and is reprinted here by kind permission of K. R. Gupta

Published in 2005 by
Routledge
Taylor & Francis Group
270 Madison Ave,
New York NY 10016

Published in Great Britain by
Routledge
Taylor & Francis Group
2 Park Square,
Milton Park, Abingdon,
Oxon, OX14 4RN

Library of Congress Cataloging-In-Publication Data

Catalog record is available from the Library of Congress

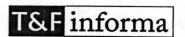

Taylor & Francis Group
is the Academic Division of T&F Informa plc.

Visit the Taylor & Francis Web site at
http://www.taylorandfrancis.com

and the Routledge Web site at
http://www.routledge-ny.com

Publisher's Note
The publisher has gone to great lengths to ensure the quality of this reprint
but points out that some imperfections in the original may be apparent

Contents

Acknowledgments

I worked on this project for sixteen months, and I am indebted to my entire graduate committee. Professors Daniel Cottom, Vincent B. Leitch, Robert Warrior, Su Fang Ng, and Jidlap Kamoche provided a challenging and supportive intellectual community and also generously gave me the leeway that enabled me to carry the project forward. I am grateful for the critical care with which they read the entire manuscript and for their detailed and insightful suggestions, both critical and appreciative. I am very grateful to the Department of English, University of Oklahoma, for the fellowship that was critical to my being able to complete this manuscript. The faculty at the University of Oklahoma provided stimulating and thought-provoking discussions that challenged and enriched my thinking. I am also grateful to the College of Fine Arts and Humanities at the University of Nebraska-Kearney for its incredible support as well as to the office of Graduate Studies and Research for awarding me the Research Services Council Grant that enabled me to put the finishing touches on this work.

I also owe much to my parents, Suraiya and Ali, whose encouragement and support have made life far pleasanter than it might have been. Last but not least, Faisal's cheeriness and patience made the task of writing this manuscript and later, my daughter Iman's luminous eyes and winsome smile made the labor of revising it a pleasant task.

Chapter One

Transporting the Subject: The Fiction of Nationality in an Era of Transnationalism

> The context of immigration can also alter the nature of the diasporic experience. The earlier diasporas of the neo-colonial and post-colonial world were often a product of forced immigration, of people running away from religious and other political or social persecution. . . . The new immigrant was a new kind of colonizer, taking full advantage of the war-time labor market, at the same time having no intention of ruling over the land. They had a home to go back to and an identity to protect; they were "resident aliens" who kept up their citizenship and indulged in, and even theorized a politics of identity. (Satchidanandan 19)

Many scholars are of the opinion that contemporary transnationalism helps usher in a new post-national era (Appadurai 12; Kumar 119; Spivak 122). But such transnationalism does not necessarily weaken nationalism; on the contrary, it can at times operate to reinforce a nationalist agenda. Despite the creation of a new global order, has not transnationalism led to the politicization of identity in the form of fundamentalism, xenophobia, and a fanatical espousal of tradition, as many critics observe? It is increasingly doubtful that transnational practices are generally counter-hegemonic. According to Michael Peter Smith and Luis Eduardo Guarnizo, transnationalism enables the fortification of nationalist ideology in two ways:

> The expansion of transnational practices has resulted in outbursts of entrenched, essentialist nationalism in both "sending" and "receiving" countries. In receiving nation-states, movements aimed at recuperating and reifying a mythical national identity are expanding as a way to eliminate the penetration of alien "others." States of origin, on the other hand, are re-essentializing their national identity and extending it to

their nationals abroad as a way to maintain their loyalty and flow of
resources "back home." (10)

Thus, the dissemination of transnational practices entails the transterritorial-
ization of various socioeconomic, political, and cultural practices and identities that frequently bolster the formation and reconstitution of the
nation-state.

As Arjun Appadurai observes, diasporic communities such as the ones
formed through the phenomenon of transnationalism in the West Indies,
Malaya, Fiji, Mauritius, Eastern and Western Africa, the U.K., and the U.S.,
"safe from the depredations of their home states . . . become doubly loyal to
their nations of origin" (49). Transnationalism implies a process in which
formations that have traditionally been perceived as restricted to well-defined
political and geographical boundaries have transgressed national borders,
producing new social formations. Yet transnational politics often lead to cultural and religious fanaticism by emphasizing a conception of identity polarized between the "authentic" and the "demonic." Exploring how South Asian
identity is negotiated in Western spaces, this chapter examines two key questions: How are transnational identities related to the invention, transmission,
and revision of nationalist histories? How do transnational practices affect
canonical understandings of literary texts?

In exploring these questions, my book focuses on the representation of
South Asian life in works by four contemporary Anglophone writers: V. S.
Naipaul, Salman Rushdie, Amitav Ghosh, and Anita Desai. Of course, I
refer to works by other writers, such as Sara Suleri, Bapsi Sidhwa, and
Khushwant Singh. Concentrating on the intertwined topics of nationalism,
transnationalism, and fundamentalism, my analysis addresses the dislocation
that is caused by the transformations associated with these phenomena. I
offer a critical dialogue between these works and the contemporary history
they encounter, using history to interrogate fiction and using fiction to think
through historical issues.

The kind of dialogue I have in mind can be exemplified by the Ram
Janmabhoomi agitation of 1989. Either directly or indirectly, the types of
conflicts that led to this event resonate throughout the writings of the
authors with whom I am concerned in this study. A disused sixteenth-
century mosque in Ayodhya, the Babri Masjid, was demolished by Hindu
supporters of the Saffron movement who hoped to construct a temple, the
Ram Janmabhoomi, on that site. Hindu-Muslim riots swept Northern India
in the wake of the Ram Janmabhoomi agitation. Both sides attempted to create a new past for the nation. In the case of the majority Hindus, the militant

Hinduism that the Ram Janmabhoomi movement incited challenged the basic principle that the nation was founded on: democracy. Community was evoked in order to create nostalgia for a concocted past that was meticulously contrived. The religious chauvinism that was manifested during this dark period in the history of India was transformed into bigotry supported by transnationals in the U.S. and the U.K. Bigotry defined identities and ideologies, treating the idea of a polyglot and polychrome nation as if it were a myth. The left-wing activists who endeavored to transform that "myth" into reality were dubbed "outsiders" and "inauthentic." These progressive attempts of left-wing activists were challenged by the construction of a mythic history asserting masculinist virility and national tradition in a classically fascist form.

This project of constructing the history of a nation involves selective appropriation of past and present histories and an abrogation of major parts of those histories. For instance, Kai Friese reports in the *New York Times* that in November 2002, during the reign of the Bharatiya Janata Party, the National Council of Education Research and Training in India, which is the central Indian government organization that finalizes the national curriculum and supervises education for high school students, circulated a new textbook for Social Sciences and History. The textbook conveniently overlooks the embarrassing fact that the architect of Indian independence, Mohandas Karamchand Gandhi, was assassinated by a Hindu nationalist in 1948, a year after the proclamation of independence. Friese makes the reader aware that this version of Indian history has also been embellished by some interesting fabrications. One of those fabrications is the erasing of the "Indus Valley" Civilization and its replacement by the mythical "Indus-Saraswati" Civilization. The erasure of the Indus Valley Civilization and the conjuring of the "Indus-Saraswati" Civilization in its stead is a strategic maneuver to negate the fact that the ancient scriptures of Hinduism are associated with the advent of the Aryan peoples from the Northwest, and that Hinduism is a syncretic religious tradition that has evolved through a commingling of various cultures and traditions (15).

In this nationalist project, one of the forms that the nullification of past and present histories takes is the subjection of religious minorities to a centralized and authoritarian state buttressed by nostalgia of a "glorious past." Thus, the Babri Masjid, an obscure little mosque, was destroyed by an unruly mob that rallied around the Bharatiya Janata Party, which is the second largest political party in India. By blatantly advocating and supporting the destruction of the Babri Masjid, the Bharatiya Janata Party and its votaries negated the legislation of the highest court of law in the land that sought to protect the site by staying its appropriation by any political party. The legislation was not only abrogated by the active mobilization of the fractious crowd, but by the bigwigs of the BJP who presided over the demolition of the mosque. This spectacle was staged as an instance of mass hysteria and bacchanalian disorder. The mob was spurred on by an overwhelming sense of hysteria and exhortations to violence. This movement, as Vijay Mishra observes, received financial support from Hindu immigrants in the West, "and the funding of Hindu institutions, temples, and other purportedly 'charitable' enterprises by diaspora Hindus, particularly those from the United States, can be established beyond doubt" (194). Such appeals and unambiguous encouragement to enjoin the native mob to commit acts of violence were, according to Aijaz Ahmad, "replete with appeals to masculine virility, national pride, racial redemption, contempt for law and civility" (*Lineages* 183).

One of the celebrities whose historical analysis of the Islamic conquests in India seems to fan the flames of divisive politics, pitting Hindus against Muslims, is the Nobel laureate, V. S. Naipaul. In his *Beyond Belief* Naipaul dismissed Islam as an alien imposition which had estranged the nations of the Indian subcontinent from their own heritage. He writes that the Muslims of India and Pakistan lack an "authentic" Muslim lineage and so are severed from a keen sense of reality. According to the author, the condition of such non-Arab Muslims has "an element of neurosis and nihilism" (*Beyond Belief* 34). Naipaul's inference seems to erase the tremendous adaptation, indigenization, and evolution of Islam in countries like India. Needless to say, it reinforces the claims of right-wingers who label present-day Muslims "outsiders" or "invaders" in India. Such claims ignore how communities grow historically within the framework created by a dialogic discourse. The author, of Indian origin who lives in England, has portrayed India as "full of the signs of growth," with all the signs of an "Indian, and more specifically, Hindu awakening" (*India* 98). Rushdie makes a slighting reference to this sympathetic attitude toward Hindu fanaticism in *The Moor's Last Sigh* and to the complicity of the bumbling Indian bureaucracy in this network of political and discursive relations, offering an example of the multifaceted dialogue of contemporary literature and history engaged by transnational writers living in the diaspora:

> The mosque at Ayodhya was destroyed. Alphabet-soupists, "fanatics," or, alternatively, "devout liberators of the sacred site" (delete according to taste) swarmed over the seventeenth-century Babri Masjid and tore it apart with their bare hands, with their teeth, with the elemental power

of what Sir V. S. Naipaul has approvingly called their "awakening to history." The police, as the press photographs showed, stood by and watched the forces of history do their history-obliterating work. (363)

Significantly, the espousal of nationalism in Naipaul's later work is ambivalent in his earlier fiction. For instance, the identity of the postcolonial subject in *Mimic Men,* who, like Naipaul himself, simultaneously attempts to straddle the cultures of the Caribbean, India, and England, is ambiguous, to say the least. The protagonist, Ralph Singh, is an ousted colonial minister who has been exiled from the Caribbean island of his birth. While in the Caribbean and then in an exiled state in England, he attempts to create a new cultural and social space by emulating the ways of the British. Ralph Singh tells the reader about the modifications made to his original name, which had an East Indian etymology, as part of this transnational process:

> We were Singhs. My father's father's name was Kirpal. My father, for purposes of official identification, necessary in that new world he adorned with his aboriginal costume, ran these names together to give himself the surname of Kripalsingh. My own name was Ranjit; and my birth certificate said I was Ranjit Kripalsingh. That gave me two names.
> . . . I broke Kripalsingh into two, correctly reviving an ancient fracture, as I felt; gave myself the further name of Ralph; and signed myself R. R. K. Singh. At school I was known as Ralph Singh. The name Ralph I chose for the sake of the initial, which was also that of my real name. In this way I felt I mitigated the fantasy or deception; and it helped in school reports, where I was simply Singh R. (Naipaul 93)

This transnational space is geographically unmoored from Ralph Singh's country of origin, and his attempt to affirm the anglicization of his name could be seen, in Homi Bhabha's terms, as underlining the dynamics of mimicry that stems from its simultaneous espousal of two diverse realities and consequent disruption of the authority of colonial discourse (88). Ralph Singh's simultaneous adherence to his legacy and to an identity that is accommodated by Britain dissolves the clear borders between the world and the home, the outside and the inside, and the public and the private. In other words, the politics of the empire include the provincial self, articulating a sensibility linked by multilayered identities and the remapping of old imperial landscapes. Such a sensibility suggests a new dynamic of power relations in which politics and selfhood, empire and psychology, prove to be profoundly interrelated. There is here an implicit disavowal of monologic nationalist identity.

Similarly, when the Indian family in Naipaul's *House for Mr. Biswas* tries to create a "home away from home" in Trinidad by preserving Indian traditions and customs, their attempt turns into a fiasco. This narrative has been classified as one of "return," an attempt to construct an imaginary Indian homeland in the Caribbean, but the traditions that Biswas's family espouses are a reconstruction of East Indian cultural practices that have been adapted to the West Indian cultural milieu. So this awareness of an originary home is a new invention of a transnational identity.

Naipaul does critique myths of origin and of national sensibility in his novels, but I would argue that these reincriptions are contradicted by a tenacious clinging to the "glorious" past of the imperial age. His refusal to question the purported glory of the British empire plays into his support of Hindu extremism and his unambiguous criticism of "Islamic imperialism": "There probably has been no imperialism like that of Islam and the Arabs. Islam seeks as an article of the faith to erase the past; the believers in the end honor Arabia alone, they have nothing to return to" (Naipaul, *Beyond Belief* 98). This belief is reiterated in an interview with Farukh Dhondy in which Naipaul blames the derelict state of the Indian polity and culture on Muslim invasions in India and on the attempt, in the teaching of the independence movement, to nullify that perception: "I went against the teaching of the independence movement that spoke of the two cultures, the two religions being one really—and I saw that India had been crushed by the Muslims" (5). While declaring these invasions as culpable acts of historical mutation, Naipaul absolves the British of historically truncating India's civilization. With examples like these in mind, I explore in Chapter Two the complexities in Naipaul's stance vis-à-vis nationalism, nationalist subjectivity, and transnationalism.

I am particularly intrigued by the exploration of the politics, culture, and religious "hysteria" inside four Islamic nations in Naipaul's *Among the Believers: An Islamic Journey*. In this travelogue, he depicts Islamic society as an anomaly in the modern world. All the four Islamic nations that Naipaul traverses are ripped apart culturally and economically by imperialism, nationalism, religious revival, and transnationalism. As he portrays it, Islamic fundamentalism in Iran, Pakistan, Indonesia, and Malaysia organizes an insidious network of social and political organizations that spreads across cultural and geographical boundaries and contributes to the rabidity of Islam. This network is oblivious to the geographical and cultural boundaries that separate nation-states from one another. As Smith and Guarnizo put it, "Politically organized transnational networks and movements also weld together transnational connections by constituting structures of meaning"

(19). For instance, while interviewing one of Ayatollah Khomeini's disciples at a religious institution in Iran, Naipaul makes the acquaintance of a group of students from Pakistan who support the unification of state and religion propounded subsequent to the ousting of the monarchical structure in Iran. This group of Pakistani students is at an Iranian religious institution in order to imbibe the way of life taught at that institution so they can propagate similar religious and political beliefs in their country of origin. In Naipaul's view, the identities that these transnational subjects forge are as essentialized as the hegemonic projects of nation-states. Thus, although these students are geographically unmoored from their country of origin, they serve to reinforce Naipaul's assumptions about the purity and fixity in religion as propagated in Iran. My analysis is devoted, in part, to a critique of those assumptions and of their consequences, both in Naipaul's writing and in the social and cultural worlds he claims to represent. In other words, I attempt to establish the process of identity formation in a transnational realm as one of perpetual struggle in which, as Smith and Guarnizo put it, "discursive communities produce narratives of belonging, resistance, or escape" (23). In this realm, writers create an interstitial space between cosmopolitan and the parochial where they might observe other resistance histories and political agendas in order to speak in a transnational discourse. At the same time, I compare Naipaul's non-fiction to his fictional works, such as *Mimic Men,* in which his attitudes toward religion, nationalism, and other topics often appear so startlingly different.

Indian-born Salman Rushdie, an author of South Asian origin, is at odds with Naipaul's take on the Ram Janmabhoomi movement and his portrayal of Islamic revivalism. Rushdie describes Naipaul's *Among the Believers* as

> a highly selective truth, a novelist's truth masquerading as reality. Take Iran: no hint in these pages that in the new Islam there is a good deal more than Khomeinism, or that the mullocracy's hold on the people is actually very fragile. . . . And what of (or have we forgotten him already?) the Shah of Iran? Naipaul quotes just two criticisms of him. . . . Are these really the only Muslims Naipaul could find to speak against the Shah?

> Terrible things are being done today in the name of Islam; but simplification of the issues, when it involves omitting everything that can't easily be blistered by Naipaul's famous Olympian disgust, is no help. At one point, Naipaul tells his friend Shafi: "I think you traveled to America with a fixed idea, you might have missed some things." The criticism holds good for Naipaul's own journey in the opposite direction, and

makes *Among the Believers,* for all its brilliance of observation and direction, a rather superficial book. (*Imaginary Homelands* 375)

Rushdie employs the markedly different method, in *The Satanic Verses,* of including repressed voices from the non-European world in order to foreground the cultural and historical perspectives external to Europe. I argue that Rushdie puts forth his cultural knowledge to generate a dialectical interplay between the voice from the non-European world and the dominant European discourse. Describing his position as a transnational subject, Rushdie says:

> It may be that writers in my position, exiles or emigrants or expatriates, are haunted by some sense of loss, some urge to reclaim, to look back, even at the risk of being mutated into pillars of salt. But if we do look back, we must also do so in the knowledge—which gives rise to profound uncertainties—that our physical alienation from India almost inevitably means that we will not be capable of reclaiming precisely the thing that was lost; that we will, in short, create fictions, not actual cities or villages, but invisible ones, imaginary homelands, Indias of the mind. ("Imaginary Homelands" 10)

In contrast to Naipaul, Rushdie encourages a nationalist self-imagining and rewriting of history that incorporates profound cultural, religious, and linguistic differences into the text, as postcolonial theorists like Bhabha and earlier Frantz Fanon claim is necessary in the process of nation-building. But Fanon's claim is more profound, according to which native resistance movements provide inspiration to one another and are cross- or transnational in their range of influence (54–5).

Since Independence, the Indian polity has undergone dislocation and restructuring, with, as Ahmad tells us, "contradictory tendencies towards greater integrative pressures of the market and the nation-state on the one hand, greater differentiation and fragmentation of communities and socio-economic positions on the other" (191). In Chapter Three, I analyze how Rushdie deploys his knowledge of history and culture to evaluate the multiplicity of contradictory discourses and influences involved in the creation of a society. However, unlike Rushdie, Naipaul examines how movements that are nationally focused in terms of their political organization may be transnational in their reception of influence. But it could be argued that both these authors privilege the relationship of European self and other, of colonizer and colonized. Contrary to Fanon's theory of native resistance movements which find instructive models in one another's agenda and experience, Naipaul and Rushdie subscribe to the conventional practice of locating the point of political and cultural exchange between the European colonial center and its peripheries instead of between peripheries.

As everyone knows, Salman Rushdie's *The Satanic Verses* caused an upheaval in the Islamic world. The furor surrounding the book incited the Shiite religious leader, Ayatollah Khomeini, to issue an edict demanding the author's head on a platter. Because of the jeopardy his life was in, Rushdie was in hiding from 1989 until 2001. The decision to ban the book was taken by some countries in order to quell the unrest that was caused by the vociferous protests of national and transnational Muslim communities against the ostensibly blasphemous "Mahound" and "Ayesha" sections (Pipes 112). Important literary and political questions arose from this affair. For instance, by writing a work of fiction in which the references to Islam seem to be deliberate attempts at blasphemy, was Rushdie merely reiterating the polarized identities created by institutionalized religion? By portraying his protagonist as a versatile mimic, was Rushdie mocking the displaced immigrant who doubles the white man's image? Or is Rushdie's characterization of Gibreel in *The Satanic Verses* as an icon of indigenous "theological" films an affirmation of ethnocentricity that resists easy decoding? How does *The Satanic Verses* compare to *Midnight's Children* and *Shame,* in which Rushdie portrays the configuration of post-Independence India and Pakistan as chaotic and unwieldy? What kind of view about the democratization of the postcolonial realm is the author offering us?

While globalization provides a key context to exploring Rushdie's fiction, it is no secret that in the age of globalization there has been an unprecedented reversion to local, fundamentalist, and fiercely anti-internationalist interests. "Honor Killings" in Pakistan and Afghanistan are caused by fierce adherence to a "traditional" code of conduct. The Hindu-Muslim conflict in India and the ethnic cleansing in Kashmir are caused by reversion to religious and regional sentiments.

My study evaluates the extent to which Naipaul and Rushdie are able to question the resurgence of this sort of sentiment and the social, cultural, and political struggles related to it. In this attempt, I also question the school of thought according to which writers from the Indian subcontinent living in the West are said to live in circumstances that are so psychologically and materially severed from those of the inhabitants of those countries on the subcontinent as to render them emotionally and spiritually, as well as physically, removed (Sahgal 8). I conclude that these writers articulate their ideologies in a voice that is "recognizable to another broader community," yet incorporate notions of their essentialized spiritual and mythic resources which they believe have not been influenced by the West (Nairn 7–8). As

Gyan Prakash summarizes it, "the unity of the national subject was forged in the space of difference and conflicts" (9–10).

The formerly colonized population of South Asia constitutes a space in which conflicting discourses have been written and read. In the present circumstances, the populace of India and other parts of South Asia have an ambivalent role in their complicity with and resistance to the forces that jeopardize their existence. Amitav Ghosh explores this ambivalence in all its complexity in *The Shadow Lines,* which I examine in Chapter Four. The peoples of the Indian subcontinent are depicted as opposing the legacy of colonialism, a wish that is expressed as a desire to liberate themselves from oppressive conditions of life by forging cross-cultural, interdiscursive, and transnational movements that are staked out across as well as within geopolitical boundaries. But as they seek to improve their lives, they find that oppositional nationalist and proto-nationalist movements can pose as dark a threat to their identities as that which colonialism presented.

To understand *The Shadow Lines,* some background is necessary. In India, the uncritical reversion to fundamentalism and the superficial creation of a "unified" political identity in the wake of nationalist movements led to an erosion of unique and distinctive cultural identities. In the post-Partition era, this threat led the Bengali people of the Indian state of West Bengal and people of the same ethnicity in East Pakistan to challenge the political structures entrenched during colonial rule and the birth of the nation. In India and Pakistan, these structures were responsible for the concentration of power in Delhi and West Pakistan, respectively, which both tended to administer foreign aid and other revenues to themselves, even though West Bengal and East Pakistan had large populations and sustained the agrarian economy in the two countries. The result of this highly centralized federation was a marginalizing of outlying states. The feeling of alienation amongst Bengalis was augmented by the proclamation of Hindi as the official language in North India and Urdu as the official language in Pakistan. According to the *Census of India, 1951,* 84.62% of the inhabitants of West Bengal have Bengali as the native language (52). The *Census of Pakistan, 1951* states that 98% of the inhabitants of East Bengal have Bengali as their mother tongue and they represent 55% of the total population of Pakistan (68). As was reported in the Pakistani newspaper, *Dawn,* in 1948, the first Prime Minister of Pakistan, Liaqat Ali Khan, responded to the suggestion that Bengali be permitted in the assembly in the following words:

> Pakistan is a Muslim state, and it must have its lingua franca, a language
> of the Muslim nation. The mover should realize that Pakistan has been

created because of the demand of a hundred million Muslims in this sub-continent, and the language of a hundred million Muslim is Urdu. It is necessary for a nation to have one language and that language can only be Urdu and no other language. (qtd. in Ahmad 112)

In a similar move in India, the Father of the Nation, Mahatma Gandhi, and the first Prime Minister, Jawaharlal Nehru, declared that a community could be forged between Hindus and Muslims by creating a "link" language that was colloquial and based on the spoken vernacular. So Hindustani was adopted as the device to transcend the pernicious Hindi-Urdu controversy (Ahmad 115). Here, too, the consequent marginalization of the Bengali language was a blow to Bengali self-definition.

These socioeconomic and cultural inequities have been re-emphasized in independent India by the launching of a far-reaching affirmative action program that ensures quotas in academic and government institutions for "scheduled" or menial castes and tribes. In the opinion of those who opposed this program, by ensuring quotas for members of scheduled castes and tribes, the nationalist government eroded the establishment of a meritocracy. Having traditionally belonged to the educated elite, Bengalis, particularly Bengali Muslims, felt aggrieved by this perceived erosion. The situation was worsened by the slow growth of the Indian economy, which limited the expansion of openings in public and private sectors, thus preventing the majority of educated people from availing themselves of job opportunities.

The resulting cultural conflict was exacerbated by the political conflict among the Muslim communities of East and West Pakistan. The people of Bengali descent in the feudally dominated state of West Bengal and in East Pakistan prided themselves on their unique cultural heritage and intellectual prowess. But Bengali Muslims in the Indian state of West Bengal and in East Pakistan were indignant because of the perceived refusal to negotiate their demands. The general perception among Bengali Muslims was that the concentration of power in Delhi, with its wealthy Punjabi industrialists, had relegated their distinct Bengali culture to the background, and they had been denied adequate political representation by both Delhi and Islamabad. The feeling of resentment was exacerbated tenfold by the division of the state of Bengal into the Hindu-dominated West Bengal and the Muslim-dominated East Pakistan.

The result was a demand for a separate nation for Bengali Muslims. The demand of nationhood was made a reality by the Indian military incursion into Pakistan in 1971. The foray of India into its neighboring country was a well-planned and strategic operation. It was the military and economic succor provided by the government of India to the Bengali separatists in East Pakistan that precipitated the creation of Bangladesh. But the citizens of the two countries were deprived of agency and millions were rendered homeless and dispossessed. Gutted homes, rivulets of blood, ravaged lands, and meaningless loss of lives were the costs of this nation-building. The upsurge of ethnic and religious fundamentalism that led to the creation of Pakistan and Bangladesh has been characterized by Ashish Nandy as a nationalism that takes its toll on a polyglot society, such as India's:

> First it comes bundled with official concepts of state, ethnicity, territoriality, security and citizenship. Once such a package captures public imagination, it is bound to trigger in the long run, in a society as diverse as ours, various forms of "subnationalism" . . . the idea of the nation in the "official" theory of nationhood can be made available in a purer form to culturally more homogeneous communities such as the Sikhs, the Kashmiri Muslims, the Gorkhas and the Tamils. As a result, once the ideology of nationalism is internalized, no psychological barrier is left standing against the concepts of new nation-states, that would be theoretically even purer, homogeneous national units—in terms of religion, language, and culture. (5)

The havoc wreaked by the kindling of Bengali nationalism is vividly portrayed by Ghosh in *The Shadow Lines*. Ghosh depicts one of the characters in the novel, who tries to bridge racial and religious divides by the relationships he forges, as one of the "collateral damages" of this nationalist movement. In his portrayal, the further division of West and East Pakistan into Pakistan and Bangladesh made amply clear the error of not attempting to transcend ethnolinguistic divides, casteism, class barriers, and religious dogmas.

The aftermath of 1971 was a period of political instability in Pakistan. The country witnessed a series of coup d'états, which were orchestrated by the army in order to establish military dictatorships. The ardent nationalism of that era led to an entrenched and centralized nation-state. Again, the further division of Pakistan and the lack of transparency in the undemocratic political set-up incited organized persecutions and massacres. *The Shadow Lines* addresses this history through the life of the narrator.

As the narrator of *The Shadow Lines* implies, neither history alone nor a single theory sufficiently frames the multiple inheritances of present diasporic subjectivities. In "The Diaspora in Indian Culture," Ghosh suggests that India does not create a sense of nationhood in her diasporas, arguing that the dislocated people of India do not carry one language as other diasporic groups had done but, on the contrary, they carry innumerable languages and religious cultures already rooted in "systematic diversity" (76). Ghosh insists that the Indian diasporic community lacks this sense of homogeneity because if "there is any one pattern in Indian culture in the broadest sense, it is that the culture has been constructed around the proliferation of differences" (77). In Chapter Four of my book, I argue that Ghosh is critical of the putative historical and religious necessity to forge a unified nationalist identity. At the same time, I argue that the resurgence of cultural and religious fanaticisms in certain transnational communities negates Ghosh's utopian view of differences, despite its historical basis.

The unease of minority communities in modern India is further explored by Anita Desai in her novel *In Custody,* the subject of my fifth chapter. The author carefully delineates the unfair treatment meted out to religious and linguistic minorities by the internal hierarchies entrenched by nationalism. For instance, the imperialism of Hindi in post-Partition India relegates the poetic language of the lost Muslim empire, Urdu, to the background. Desai's novel highlights the issues of poetry in a particular language in relation to an array of matters: political power, ethnicity, religion, religious prejudice, and other problems permeating the Indian subcontinent. Ahmad explains the decline of Urdu literature and poetry in post-Partition India succinctly:

> Independence and Partition were doubtless key watersheds in the chequered history of the Urdu language and its literature, in the sense that the thematic of this literature as well as the reading and writing communities were fragmented and recomposed drastically, in diverse ways (103).

As Desai portrays it, the moribund state that Urdu finds itself in is symbolic of the decadence and decrepitude of Muslim culture in a Hindu-majority nation. As Prabhu S. Guptara summarizes the final phase of the nationalist movement: "Having got rid of the English, the paradoxical Indians turned to their language with a remarkable passion: our Constitution, adopted in 1951, was written in English, and recognized two official languages, English and Hindi, which the government had made determined efforts to promote" (24). Subsequent to 1947, the year India proclaimed itself an independent nation, Muslim culture was metaphorically dislocated. In other words, it can be argued that Muslim culture suffered a psychological denigration. In this context, the dislocation of migrancy foregrounds the issues of language, voice, and translation.

In contrast to this English-Hindi dominance, the world of Urdu literature in the novel is portrayed as a domain of male friendships in which the male narrator deifies the Urdu poet, Nur, and is leery of the poet's talented wife, whose attempts to wax eloquent are perceived as an incursion into a carefully guarded male domain. The narrator dons the mantle of Nur's confidante, but his sense of responsibility does not extend to the poet's wives, who are rendered destitute subsequent to their husband's death. Meanwhile, the narrator's wife is the keeper and perpetuator of the spiritual dimension of the nation and its microcosmic representation, the home. She awaits the day her dreams of "fan, phone, frigidaire" will be fulfilled.

It could be argued that Desai portrays the world of male friendship in order to demonstrate how this is a part of the process that reproduces the native woman's victimization. Or is her unrelenting critique of the snobbishness of Muslim culture an attempt to usher in a post-national era in which sterile and dysfunctional aspects of a culture are excised in order to dispel nostalgic nationalist myths? Or could Desai actually be advocating a unitary politics of nationalism that glosses over ethnolinguistic and cultural divides? I look at *In Custody* as providing a framework that enables an inquiry into cultures and societies, an inquiry in which Desai seeks to imagine a responsible form of artistic, social, and political agency. This novel evokes particular interest because of the resurgence of militant Hindu nationalism in modern India and the accompanying dominance of Hindi as the official language.

The authors whose works I focus on are of South Asian origin. All four straddle several worlds, geographically, culturally, and politically. V. S. Naipaul espouses Indian, Trinidadian, and British cultures; British-educated Salman Rushdie was one of the people dispossessed by the exodus of Muslims from India after the Partition; Amitav Ghosh is of Bengali and Burmese origin; Anita Desai is of Indian and German origin. Three of these authors, Naipaul, Rushdie, and Ghosh, have chosen the West as their territory of adoption. Fittingly, their works deal with the processes of acculturation. The works of these authors delineate the asymmetrical relations of colonialism and the aftermath of this phenomenon as it is manifested across the globe in this day and age. Not only do these authors address the transfer of culture from the centers of domination to the colonies, but they also speak to the spilling over of metropolitan modes of representation into the self-construction of the colonized and the formerly colonized. A related issue addressed in works I have chosen is that of the fabrication of a new past for the nation.

Despite their differences, all four authors have attempted to retrieve histories that have been distorted or erased in discourses of power. *Among the Believers, The Satanic Verses, The Shadow Lines,* and *In Custody* seek to explore the disrupting and disorienting consequences of dislocation. Does dislocation enable the regeneration of cultural forces? Does it entail a cultural and psychological denigration? Does dislocation offer just two alternatives, transnational identity or a tenacious holding on to origins? Does transnationalism enable a reconstruction respectful of cultural differences? Does it, as is often claimed, allow subjects to "engage in reflexive self-critical distancing from their own cultural discourses, and hence also to recognize the potential validity of other discourses/communities of language" (Werbner 14)? Do the cosmopolitan political and cultural ideologies of Naipaul, Rushdie, Ghosh, and Desai, in fact, challenge ethnocentric cultural assumptions? I explore these questions in the contexts of geographical and cultural dislocation, the Ram Janmabhoomi movement in India, the furor caused in the entire Islamic world by Rushdie's novel, the political and cultural ideologies attending the war of 1971, the disillusioning failure of certain narratives of national liberation, and the assumed hegemony of "Hindu pride" symbolized by the demolition of the Babri Masjid in India.

In doing so, I argue that in the mixed, heterogeneous space of transnationalism, cultural and linguistic authenticity is a pipe dream. The binary structures created by the colonial encounter undergo a process of dialectical interplay in which each culture or language makes incursions into the other. Their recognition of this dialogic continuity of community and place becomes the basis for strategies that enable transnational and postcolonial writers to revise dogmatic categories:

> ... the critical position that would see the English Canadian, or for that matter any postcolonial culture's, literary tradition as "discontinuous," one in which writers find no "usable past" in the apparently colonized literary productions of earlier times, may itself be blind to modes of continuity that can prevail beneath the surface of established generic classifications. (Slemon 422)

By mingling the phantasmic and the plausible, transnational writers often "demand the prerogative of 'redreaming their own land'" (Slemon 419). Instead of a contemptuous dismissal of the power of myth and fetishes, these writers explore these narratives and beliefs as repositories of culture. This process of recuperation makes the hitherto lost voices of the margins audible, voices such as those of South Asian and black diasporas as lived within Britain. The pluralistic visions of the world that this writing suggests shows how the process of transnationalism engenders "unhomeliness—that is the condition of extra-territorial and cross-cultural initiation" (Bhabha 34). Salman Rushdie says of this process of adaptation, assimilation, appropriation, and hybridization,

> I am no longer Indian in the way that I would be if I hadn't left, I'm another thing. For a long time I would try and tell myself that this wasn't

> so, and that somehow that was still Home, and this [England] was still
> away. When I went back there I was going home. It's true that even now I
> feel 'at home' in Bombay, in particular, in a way I don't feel anywhere else
> in the world really. But I came to feel that I had to stop telling myself that:
> that there was a sense in which it had become a fiction that was no longer
> useful to me: it was a way of not looking at the real things about my life,
> which were that that isn't home, that that is away. This [England] is
> home. In a way, you can't go home again. (qtd. in Hamilton 96)

Rushdie's avowal of cultural eclecticism is unequivocal in *The Satanic Verses*.
He advocates the formation of composite identities, and deploys the process
of cultural "hybridity" to create positions for reconstruction. Rushdie's
emphasis on "composite identities" suggests that diasporic subjectivities have
emerged from diverse subject positions and varied historical and cultural
contexts. But is his appropriation of the language of the dominant power in
fact an attempt to reconceive culture and society so that the "trans-historic-
ity" of colonialism and its aftermath does not neutralize the subjectivity of
indigenous peoples (Gandhi 169).

   In order to assume agency in transnational realms, Naipaul, Ghosh,
and Desai, like Rushdie, have inverted the dominant representation of formerly colonized cultures as degenerate. They reject the interpretive practices that painted the people of the East as epitomizing "heathen
incorrigibility" that ought to be repressed. In doing so, these authors construct narratives that derive from an eclectic range of literary and cultural
intertexts, and from histories that are both complicit and resistant. In this
process of nationalist self-imagining, post-independence narrative is a self-
conscious rewriting of history and of the creation of symbols of nationhood, a rewriting derived from the cross-cultural influences of the authors'
vexed individual diasporic conditions:

> The Indian writer, looking back at India, does so through guilt-tinted
> spectacles. (I am, of course once more, talking about myself). I am
> speaking now of those of us who emigrated and I suspect that there are
> times when the move seems wrong to us all, when we seem to our-
> selves postlapsarian men and women. We are Hindus who have
> crossed the black water; we are Muslims who eat pork. . . . We are now
> partly of the West. Our identity is at once plural and partial. Some-
> times we feel that we straddle two cultures; at other times, we fall
> between two stools but however ambiguous and shifting this ground
> may be, it is not an infertile territory for a writer to occupy. (Rushdie,
> "The Indian Writer" 79)

Typically, the transformations effected by the transnational writers involve rebirths and renamings in the realms of language and the imagination. As Rushdie articulates, the "migrant" becomes the "midwife" of language itself, "as that language is new delivered," because by making incursions into an alien language, the migrant is required to traverse new territories and discover "new ways of describing himself, new ways of being human" (*Imaginary Homelands* 24).[1]

Often, in order to fortify the attempt to find new ways of delineating his or her situation, the transnational writer appropriates and adapts the language of the nation of adoption to define the reality of a different culture. The adapted form of the English language creates a linguistic medium of a syncretic character. The metamorphosis in the English language effected by the incorporation of variance into it erodes the concept and use of Standard English, thereby halting the perpetuation of a hegemonic rhetoric in culture and literature. The development of English into the vernacular form privileges the experience of a submerged voice that breaks the shackles of the "standard": "English is adopted as the national language, so its local development into vernacular form is one of both evolution and adaptation" (Ashcroft et al. 56). In its evolved form, "English" challenges the traditional culture/modern civilization binary by establishing itself as an oppositional discourse that does not unquestioningly accept the dominance of the "norm." The deployment of this oppositional discourse enables the writer to incorporate untranslated words or events of local significance in the text, requiring the reader to delve into the intricacies of a hitherto unknown culture.

As Smith and Guarnizo put it, the place of the local tradition is no longer perceived "as a derogatory site that compounds backwardness," but, on the contrary, is redefined "as a dynamic source of alternative cosmopolitanisms and contestation" (11). Such language is "a constant demonstration of the dynamic possibilities available to writing within the tension of 'center' and 'margin'" (Ashcroft et al. 59). Writers create a site on which local thought-patterns, structures, and rhythms are accompanied by the delineation of an alternative social reality. Their writing not only coins neologisms, but also incorporates indigenous languages and dialects that are signifiers of the local as opposed to the universal. The sustained opposition between the two opposing discursive systems prevents the transnational text from conforming to a restrictive system of representation.[2]

In the 1950s and 1960s, the Indian writer in English attempted to affiliate Indian writing with the dominant forms of the English novel. The generation of Naipaul and Desai did not make a serious endeavor to either explore indigenous narrative forms or to appropriate the English language to the Indian context (Narayan and Mee 220). In these writings, the social, cultural, and political realms are often places of disillusionment and enable the analysis of individual aberrations. Shyamala A. Narayan and Jon Mee observe about this generation of Indian writers, "What these novelists did demonstrate was a command of the right of Indian novelists to be taken seriously in terms of the criteria of Western novel-writing. Perhaps this represents a building up towards the cultural capital so conspicuously consumed by the Rushdie generation of the 1980s and 1990s" (231).

The 1980s witnessed a renaissance in Indian writing in English. Rushdie and Ghosh belong to this generation of writers who challenge the idea of national unity and the integrity of the nation-state. These writers endeavor to narrate the history of the nationalist struggle in a form that negates colonial historiography. The Indian novel in English in the 1980s incorporates memory, imagination, and folk-tale into sanctioned history and is skeptical about the stability of the nation and its symbols. As Mee observes about the writing of this generation of Indian novelists, "It has been deployed to call the globalization of culture to local account, to foreground the difficulties of translation and the possibilities of dialogue" (336).

The thematization of social relations is also affected by the linguistic innovations of authors whose works I analyze. As Smith and Guarnizo put it, "The social construction of 'place' is still a process of local meaning-making, territorial specificity, juridical control, and economic development, however complexly articulated these localities become in transnational economic, political, and cultural flows" (12). In other words, (a) although the text bears reference to regional realities, it still is metonymic of the transnational culture in its entirety; (b) the time frame of the novel is a metaphoric representation of the interminable process of colonization and its aftermath; and (c) the text foregrounds the canonical assumptions of both the center and the margins, destabilizing them. However, celebration of dislocation as the contentious site where psychological and spiritual emancipation might be achieved, like universalizing the detached position of an exile, has been attacked for its lack of affiliation with the indigenous politics in the Indian subcontinent.

Moreover, transnational writers like Rushdie, Naipaul, and Ghosh have been censored for a secular and liberal stance, linked to a global grammar of postmodernist and postcolonial mainstream (Appignanesi and Maitland 53). Rushdie's anti-essentialist politics of representation has been accused of undermining "the oppositional force of postcolonial politics" itself (Krishnaswamy 128). In response to such criticisms, I examine the local constraints and social moorings that affect the practices of transnational writers. In this study, I look at the historical and religious forces involved in the forging of a nationalist identity and at the consequent repositioning of the postcolonial subject.

Chapter Two

World Borders, Political Borders in Naipaul's *Among the Believers*

> You should be able to see the lineaments of today's society in the work
> of a good writer. . . . I just feel that we are living in such an interesting
> world. One must capture all the interest of this period. I don't believe
> that the world has all been written about. The world is so new.
> (Naipaul, qtd. in Gussow 20)

In his interview in the millennium special issue of *Outlook* magazine, V. S. Naipaul dismisses the idea that Indian culture is fluid and syncretic: "To say that India has a secular character is being historically unsound. Dangerous or not, Hindu militancy is a corrective to the history I have been talking about. It is a creative force and will be so. Islam can't reconcile with it" (UNI). Naipaul discounts the evolution of Hinduism and Islam as syncretic religious traditions that have developed through a commingling of cultures and traditions from various lands.

His stance echoes that of the Bharatiya Janata Party in India, which is critical of the historical scholarship establishing that the ancient scriptures of Hinduism are associated with the advent of the Vedic Aryan peoples from the Northwest. They abhor the implication that Hinduism is a syncretistic religious tradition. Writing about this anti-historical attitude, Kai Friese reported in the *New York Times* that in November 2002, the National Council of Education Research and Training, which is the central Indian government organization that finalizes the national curriculum and supervises education for high school students, circulated a new textbook for Social Sciences and History. The textbook conveniently overlooks the embarrassing fact that the architect of Indian independence, Mohandas Karamchand Gandhi, was assassinated by a Hindu nationalist in 1948, a year after the proclamation of independence. Friese also makes the reader aware that

Indian history has been embellished by some interesting fabrications. One of the fabrications is the erasure of the Indus Valley civilization and its replacement by the mythical "Indus-Saraswati" civilization. The erasing of the Indus Valley civilization and the conjuring of the "Indus-Saraswati" civilization in its stead is a strategic maneuver to transform a historical into a mythical civilization. Friese points out that the chapter on Vedic civilization lacks important dates and is inundated with uncorroborated "facts," such as those in this passage: "India itself was the original home of the Aryans. The Aryans were an indigenous race and the creators of the Vedas" (15).

Naipaul's argument overlooks these historical fabrications and reinforces the picture of Islam painted by both Islamist and Hindu fundamentalist politics. The consequences of Naipaul's carelessness in such matters of historical explanation are serious. On the one hand, he presents himself as a critic of Islamic nationalism and fundamentalism and so, at times, can seem to resemble an advocate of secular democracy like Edward W. Said. On the other hand, he adopts an image of Islam that is created by the very fundamentalism he deplores, and so his criticism, quite unlike Said's, comes to look like simple prejudice.

Naipaul's examination of four Islamic nations in *Among the Believers* (1981) attempts to come to terms with a transnational practice, Islam, constituted within historically and geographically specific points of origin and migration. The specific religion and the specific local and national contexts in which it is practiced shape the affiliations migrants can fashion with their countries of origin. For while transnational practices do traverse two or more national territories, they are forged within the enclosed spaces of "specific social, economic, and political relations which are bound together by perceived shared interests and meanings" (Stock 40). This issue of context generates an interesting question regarding relations created by transnational practices. Are transnational relations exclusively a first-generation practice?

The opposite is true, I argue. As Matthew F. Jacobson points out in writing about the diasporic identities of Irish, Polish, and Russian immigrants in the United States, "immigrant nationalisms did not simply go to the grave with the members of the migrating generation; on the contrary, a cultural thread links the diasporic political vision of the immigrants with the ethnic gestures of their grandchildren and great-grandchildren" (5). Specifically, in relation to my concerns here, the transnational connections between the politics of Islamic fundamentalism and the culture of Islamic diasporas endure. Most Muslims in Iran, Pakistan, Malaysia, and Indonesia still profess spiritual allegiance to the "uncontaminated" or "untransmogrified" form of Islam that was founded in Arabia in the seventh century A.D.[1]

In the first section of *Among the Believers,* "Iran: The Twin Revolutions," Naipaul writes about an Indian Muslim, Mr. Jaffrey, who had migrated to Iran, the heartland of Shiite Islam:

> It was Mr. Jaffrey who had introduced me to the queer logic—as queer to me at the end of my journey as it had been at the beginning—of the Islamic revival. Speaking of the injustices of Iran, Mr. Jaffrey had said he had begun to feel, even in the Shah's time, that 'Islam was the answer.' This had puzzled me. Religious assertion as an answer to political problems? Why not work for fair wages and the rule of the law? Why work for Islam and the completeness of belief? (427)

Naipaul learns, the notion that social tensions and weaknesses can be redressed by an essential culture generated by Islam and by the interplay of national, subnational, and supranational loyalties end up fortifying religious fundamentalism in national and transnational communities. Consequently, its logic is rigid and culturally insensitive, like Mr. Jaffrey's. The issue of transnationalism with which I am concerned goes beyond the distinction between religion and politics, however, and it also goes beyond the travels of specific migrants.

In the context of the revival of Islamic fundamentalism in Iran, Pakistan, Malaysia, and Indonesia, its religious and political practices are clearly not limited to those transmigrants who traverse two or more national territories. As Emmanuel S. Nelson observes, this transnational social field may be (and is) reproduced by "the continuous flow of ideas and information provided by global media, ethnic tourism, and religious and secular festivals or rituals. All these mechanisms have played a role in the re-emergence of transnational ties" (89). The movement in Iran, for instance, accomplished its goal of dethroning the monarchy and imposing a fundamentalist regime with the aid of the following factors: financial contributions from its diasporized minorities; technological changes in the means of communication; the global phenomenon of insurgent movements in Afghanistan, Palestine, and Iraq claiming to resist their former imperial rulers, with which it allied itself; and the growth of social networks expediting transnational migration and its concomitant political and economic organization (Weiss 149).

An example that Naipaul provides of the pivotal role played by transnational flows (Appadurai 1996) is the Iranian hostage crisis that occurred in 1980. A group of students who called themselves "Muslim students following the line of Khomeini" held a party of Americans hostage inside the American embassy in Tehran, the capital of Iran. This crisis created a stir not only in the global media, which was frenetically covering the event, but also nationwide in Iran. These militant students were "critical of everybody; they were using embassy documents to make 'revelations' about everybody; they had even made 'revelations' about the *Tehran Times*" (427). The *Tehran Times* was a local English newspaper, the publication and circulation of which had been seriously undermined by the hostage crisis in Iran. This hostage crisis involved taking an action, making decisions, and developing affiliations within social networks that connected two societies, Iranian and American, simultaneously. The drama of the besieged American embassy evoked, Naipaul notes, other revolutions: "Vietnam, Africa, Nicaragua: the late-twentieth-century causes to which these Muslim students wished to attach their own cause" (422). These students advocated the ousting of monarchical rule by the Islamic Revolution that, in fact, took the country by storm once the exiled Ayatollah Khomeini returned as the triumphant leader of the insurgent movement.

The successful installation of the Islamic regime of the Ayatollah in place of the regal despotic regime of the Shah unleashed an anti-West senti-ment that knew no bounds. This movement politicized the population of Iran and instigated it to reject the derogatory representation of non-Western peoples that had been used to validate the global expansion of the two super-powers, the Soviet Union and the United States of America. The epistemol-ogy surrounding the Islamic Revolution did not require validation either from the modern West or from other parts of the post-colonial East. Thus, in order to assert his authority, the Ayatollah waged a war of symbolic utter-ances against "the leaders of some of the Christian countries who are sup-porting the tyrant shah with their Satanic power." He reinforced his position by declaring that "when the government is a Muslim and a national one, the enemy is busy plotting against us" (10). With this kind of rhetoric the Aya-tollah and his cohorts attempted to establish a system of domination based on hegemonic constructions of a transnational Muslim identity.

In this regard, Jean Baudrillard's analysis of the role played by the Ayatol-lah subsequent to the dethroning of the Iranian monarch is worth quoting:

> The Ayatollah had but one weapon at his disposal, yet that weapon, though it had no material reality, came close to being the absolute weapon: the principle of Evil. The negation of all Western values—of progress, rationality, political ethics, democracy, and so on. . . . [W]e can-not fail to recognize the superiority that his posture assures him over a West where the possibility of evoking Evil does not exist and every last trace of negativity is smothered by the virtual consensus that prevails. Our political authorities themselves are but mere shadows of their declared functions. For power exists solely by its symbolic ability to designate the

Other, the Enemy, what is at stake, what threatens us, what is Evil. (82–3)

Baudrillard designates the symbolic power of the Ayatollah as the revenge of the "Third World." The political strategy of the Ayatollah is to assert his power within a national structure in order to influence identities, fields of action, and ideologies that are not confined to the boundaries of any one single polity. Baudrillard attempts to decode the Ayatollah's motivations by pointing out that he spurns the western concepts of reason, rationality, and moral and political ethics: "By rejecting the universal consensus on all these Good Things, Khomeini became the recipient of the energy of Evil, the Satanic energy of the rejected, the glamour of the accursed share" (82). This, as Baudrillard sees it, is the challenge of the Third World, forcing the First World to pick up the gauntlet. He points out,

> The Third World has never [before] been able to throw down a real challenge to the West. As for the USSR, which for several decades incarnated Evil for the West, it is obviously in the process of quietly lining up on the side of Good, on the side of an extremely moderate way of managing things. (83)

Baudrillard makes the reader aware of the irony implicit in the role that the USSR assumed of interceding between the West and the "Satan of Tehran" by reinforcing Western values during its incursion into Afghanistan in the 1980s. The politics of the Ayatollah marked the resurgence of sentiments that were considered extinct. They resurfaced with a vengeance. I would point out that the irony that Baudrillard underlines for his readers has been further twisted in recent years given George Bush's frequent recourse to "evil" as a term for terrorists, Saddam Hussein, Al-Qaeda, Iran, and North Korea. There seems to be a territorializing of social identities at work in such discourse, an attempt to contain ethnic, subnational, supranational, and transnational identities that provide an alternative focus of loyalty to the nation-state.

Yet Naipaul does not take into consideration that at a time of political and social upheaval the consciousness of place may also offer a critical perspective from which to formulate alternatives to an insulated modernity and its concomitant political defeatism of Third-World nations. This critical perspective can be attributed to the general increase in struggles for self-determination and independence toward the end of the cold-war era. Gabriel Sheffer, professor of Political Science at the Hebrew University of Jerusalem, observes that, "during that period, the stateless Armenian diaspora more persistently and militantly pursued its goals; the Iraqi and Turkish

Kurds, strongly supported by radical elements in their diaspora in Europe, escalated their struggle against their oppressors; and Palestinians in Gaza and the West Bank launched the first Intifada, supported by various groups in their diaspora around the world" (207). Situations of political oppression and hopelessness create awakenings amongst members of their respective diasporas, enabling the processes of liberalization and democratization. In some cases, these developments enrich their homelands in cultural, political, and economic terms. Claims such as those made by Naipaul ignore how communities can grow historically within the framework created by the combined forces of modern national and transnational developments.

Naipaul's attitude could be attributed to his notion of Indian civilization, which attempts to assert a fixed identity, reinforcing the idea of the purity of culture. Susan Spearey suggests that in his fiction:

> Naipaul registers the liberation afforded by the demise of British imperial sensibility and nationalist culture, and situates himself between old worlds and new, but he continues to eschew notions of community, of active mobilization, and thus focuses on efforts on bringing as much of the old into the new as he is capable of doing. (156)

The uncritical immersion into one's indigenous cultural reality, which Naipaul's response to the Hindutva Movement endorses, is a negation of an understanding "of the variety of affective responses to the past, responses shaped by one's location" (Mohanty 233). To label the demolition of the Babri Masjid as tangible evidence of the creative force of a mass movement is to deny the existence of such a variety of responses that invests the power of choice in an individual. Since the mid-80s, rational thinkers in academia have perceived the rise of Hindu fundamentalism an attack on secular forces and as a heinous way to perpetuate the dominance of the upper castes in India. For fundamentalist organizations, religion is meant to be a hostile and vindictive force that ignores art and tradition.

Although the Ayatollah positioned himself politically against Western control, he shrewdly tried to disseminate his authoritarianism into a system of cultural and religious respect. Naipaul notes his address to "the Christians of the world," in which the Ayatollah bestows "the blessings and greetings of Almighty God to the Blessed Jesus, his glorious mother. . . . Greetings to the clergy. . . . The freedom-loving Christians" (10). While conceding the dominance of the predominantly Christian Western world, the Ayatollah asserted his intervention into the power structures of the West as well as into the predominantly Sunni Islamic world.

Although Naipaul is able to understand the Ayatollah's attempt to create an absolutist ethics that would enable him to be the interpreter of God's will, he is unable to reconcile himself to the affiliations that the Islamic Revolution seeks to forge. He admits that "the mimicry of the revolutionary motifs of the late twentieth century—the posters that appeared to celebrate peasants and urban guerillas, the Che Guevara outfits of the Revolutionary Guards—made it more unsettling" (10–11). This "mimicry" seems to have been an attempt to make common cause with other insurgent movements that struggled against their former imperialist masters. I attribute the author's discomfiture to his inability to reconcile himself to Khomeini's "new Islamic world order," in which diasporized minorities and the play between national, ethnic, and individual identities bolster the vulgarity, as Naipaul sees it, of radical clericalism.

The Ayatollah's dictatorial regime was fortified by diasporic groups. In Iran as elsewhere, these communities have been incorporated into national markets and national polities, because political and cultural elites in less industrialized societies have found that as emigration to the West has increased, the monetary transfers made by transmigrant investors have made significant contributions to their previously flagging national economies (Guarnizo and Smith 8). These significant monetary remittances benefited the Ayatollah's cause and enabled him to make use not just of symbolic force, but also of modern technology. Bernard Lewis classifies the Islamic Revolution in Iran as "the first truly modern revolution of the electronic age": "Khomeini was the first charismatic orator who sent his oratory to millions of his compatriots at home on cassettes; he was the first revolutionary leader in exile who directed his followers at home by telephone, thanks to the direct dialing that the Shah had introduced in Iran and that was available to him in France" (49). Again, elaborating on the strategic maneuvers employed by the Ayatollah, Baudrillard wrote in 1990, "The Ayatollah's strategy is a remarkably modern one, whatever people might prefer to think. Far more modern than our own, in fact, because it consists in subtly injecting archaic elements into a modern context" (84). But this alternative worldview does not necessarily create a dialogue between tradition and modernity.

Naipaul clarifies this division between tradition and modernity in Iran by pointing out that although Islam provided stability to the faithful by forging a sense of belonging, it did not offer any political or practical solutions to the issues of inequity and dominance that it raised. He critiques the identity that Islamic revivalism constructs: "To the political issues it raised it offered no political or practical solution. It offered only faith. It offered only the Prophet, who would settle everything—but who had ceased to exist. This political Islam was rage, anarchy" (355). Naipaul's view is endorsed by a seminarian, Mohammad Mojtahed Shabestari, educated in Qom, who points out that "The meaning of perfection of religion (Ekmal e Din) is not that it contains everything under the sun, so that if we were unable to find a specific item in it, we could go off calling it imperfect. It is not perfection for religion to function as a substitute for science, technology, and human deliberation" (234). In contrast to views such as Shabestari's, Khomeini ordered religious scholars in the Islamic republic to subordinate political institutions to Islamic goals and precepts, and to assume legislative, executive, and judicial positions within the republic (237). The aim of his political philosophy was to create a prescriptive system of knowledge.

The symbolic force of Khomeini's declaration of the Islamic revolution not only brought about a metamorphosis in the determinate concepts of Iranian culture but also created a situation wherein the transnational Muslim subject was forced to confront Khomeini's new Islamic world order. In other words, although his political philosophy suggested an alternative epistemology to Western rationality, it was one that did not allow negotiation between different value systems. This rigidity rends the consciousness of the transnational Muslim subject, who is caught in the quandary of living his or her life in the constant epistemological tension of having to take more than one reality system into account. For some, this diasporic consciousness can lead to alienation from one's nation of origin; for others, it can lead to an espousal of fundamentalist Islam as a way to find meaning in their origins.

Naipaul delineates this painful split in diasporic consciousness for his readers. He describes how his interest in Iran was first piqued through a reading of Nahid Rachlin's novel *The Foreigner.* The narrator, Feri, is an Iranian educated in the U.S. and married to an American university professor. She returns to Iran for a short vacation and is astonished by the incredible changes she witnesses in Tehran: "the city she goes back to is full of cars and 'Western' buildings" (14). Although this change disorients Feri, she comes to the conclusion that her salvation lies behind the veil, in a retreat into the realm of religion and spirituality. Feri's choice is the antithesis of Naipaul's choice of perpetual exile, critical distance, and religious skepticism/atheism.

From a different perspective, this Islamic hegemony, however, is also challenged by Naipaul's Iranian interpreter, Behzad, who pledges allegiance to the tenets of Communism and is disgruntled by the decrepitude that followed in the wake of the Islamic Revolution. He labels the Ayatollah a "petit bourgeois" and is convinced that "the workers and the lower classes are living under the same conditions. Nothing has changed for them. . . . They are going to start the whole system again and they're going to call it Islamic"

(416). Behzad expresses his disgruntlement in a way that neither acknowledges nor openly challenges the premise on which the Islamic regime is built, which is the subordination of political institutions to Islamic precepts and criteria determined by the ruling clerical elite. But Behzad's poignant awareness that the revolution of his dreams had turned into a nightmare for those on the left is a recognition of the tyranny of the Ayatollah's constructions of Islamic faith and identity.

Naipaul's critical stance embodies the politics of Western secularism with which he identifies. I agree with Eugene Goodheart, who is critical of Naipaul's negative stance in all his work, "What is the appeal of this virtuoso of the negative? Every scene in V. S. Naipaul's work is the occasion for mandarin scorn. It doesn't matter whether the scene is the half-developed or mimic societies of the Caribbean or the abysmal material squalor of India or the cruel places in Africa where revolutions are being made or, for that matter, the advanced societies of the West. Naipaul encounters one and all with a cold-eyed contempt" (244). In his travelogue, the author candidly admits that the doctrine of Islam did not lure him because, after all, the glories of this religion were ancient history and, in his opinion, had not evolved enough to be applicable in the modern age of science and technology (12). The author is particularly struck by the contradictions in the attitudes of young Iranians studying in the United States, like the student who declaims on the perfection of Islamic law while studying American jurisprudence at an American educational institution. Naipaul wonders, "What had attracted these Iranians to the United States and the civilization it represented?" He draws the inference that these students are drawn to the West by "more than a need for education and skills. But the attraction wasn't admitted; and in that attraction, too humiliating for an old and proud people to admit, there lay disturbance—expressed in dandyism, mimicry, boasting, and rejection" (13).

Horace B. Davis's concept of nationalism would be applicable to this professedly exclusionary nationalism within Iranian diasporic groups as well as to the coincidence of technological growth and nationalist sentiments in Iran. Professor Davis, a leftist intellectual and writer on economics, politics, and sociology, sees nationalism in non-Western areas as being spurred on by the desire for modernization (67). By positioning itself against (former) imperial countries, the Islamic Revolution developed into a coherent political movement.

Naipaul observes, "Technology surrounded us in Tehran and some of it had been so Islamized or put to such good Islamic use that its foreign origin seemed of no account" (32–33). He also notes that Iranians speak of U.S.-built fighter planes matter of factly, as though they were "as international as swords, part of the stock of the great world bazaar" (37–8). The author points out that although the Islamic regime in Iran claims to uphold the professed union of the state and religion in Islam, this union was an illusion: "The Kurds in the northwest were in rebellion; the Arabs in the southwest were restive" (35).

Naipaul is told by Mr. Jaffrey, the Indian Muslim who had migrated to Iran in order to embrace the core values of clericalism and to redress the political problems created by monarchical rule, that initially he migrated to Pakistan from India because he felt, being a Muslim, he did not have a stable future in post-partition India. Once in Pakistan, however, he realized that being a member of the Shia sect, which has been a persecuted minority in Pakistan, he would be stymied from making strides in his field. So the only alternative that was left to him was to migrate to Iran. But subsequent to the Revolution, Mr. Jaffrey was harassed by self-doubt. Although he had been an ardent supporter of Ayatollah Khomeini during the Revolution, he was suddenly besieged by worries regarding the validity of the Ayatollah's claim to the highest office. Jaffrey was of the opinion that "during the rule of the Shah the alternatives had become simple: religion or atheism," but now that the law of the Faithful had been restored, Jaffrey advocates the creation of a polity which could be established "by getting the mullahs back into the mosques, getting Khomeini to stand down, and putting politicians and administrators into the administration" (30). For individuals who propound such opinions, the kind of medieval scholarship that is institutionalized in the holy city of Qom is considered defunct, because its leaders are not modern scholars but "figure[s] of high medieval learning" (70).

Jaffrey's opinions were shaped, I argue, by his perception that as a migrant transnational subject in a globalized economy he needed to embrace cultural pluralism and a cosmopolitan syncretism. Although this perception constitutes a transnational social field and enables a reconceptualization of culture and society, it is yet riddled with contradictions and paradoxes: "Through these seemingly contradictory experiences, transmigrants actively manipulate their identities and thus both accommodate to and resist their subordination within a global capitalist system" (Glick Schiller et al. 12). An example of the resistance to subordination within a global capitalist system would be the one I mentioned in Chapter One, that of the group of Pakistani students who are in the holy city of Qom to learn the way of life being taught and perpetuated in post-Revolutionary Iran. Unlike Jaffrey, this group of students aspires to translate the political and social position gained in this political setting into political and social capital in their country of origin, Pakistan.

As in this case, instead of resulting in a liberatory discourse, transnational social fields can serve to emphasize, reinforce, or create cultural myopia and monologic identities. This deleterious short-sightedness has resulted in religious and ethno-national diasporas being faced with sporadic incidents of xenophobia within as well as against diasporic peoples. As noted by Walker Conner, Professor of Political Science and author of several books and articles on nationalism, recent large-scale Chinese and South Asian immigration to Malaysia and East Africa, respectively, seems to have prodded the rise of nativism:

> The important point is that the populated world is subdivided into a series of perceived homelands to which, in each case, the indigenous ethno-national group is convinced it has a profound and exclusive proprietary claim. (18)

But in another part of the world, the Indian subcontinent, a nation was carved by brutally and arbitrarily rending an ethno-national group into two and creating a blood-stained dichotomy. Naipaul observes in the second section of his travelogue, "Pakistan: The Salt Hills of a Dream," that Sir Mohammad Iqbal's concept of a Muslim polity was based on the premise that in addition to being an ethical ideal, Islam is a way of life inextricably linked to the social order that it fashions. The author points out Iqbal's argument maintained that the disavowal of an Islamic social order would necessarily involve a denial of the religious ideal of Islam. Therefore, "the construction of a polity on national lines, if it means a displacement of the Islamic principle of solidarity, is simply unthinkable to a Muslim" (89). Naipaul quotes an article that was published in the *Tehran Times* on the nature of Islamic polity: "How the world works is the concern of science, and how society is to be governed is the affair of politicians, but what the whole thing means is the main concern of Iran and Pakistan. Politics is combined with religion in Islam" (85). I observe that the implosion of spheres in Islamic polity is opposed to the now classic definition of Western modernity which is autonomy of spheres.

Since its creation, Pakistan has defined itself as a theocratic nation in which Muslims would be enabled to lead their lives in conformity with the tenets of Islam (Mortimer 186). The notion of a separate Indian Muslim homeland as a historical and religious necessity enabled the forging of a nationalist identity. This "theoretical fiction" deploys an essentialism to fabricate the idea of a sovereign subject. The indigenous Muslim elite of the Indian subcontinent engendered a nationalist discourse which repositioned the subject so that nation and nationalism became key concepts. I observe that this application of a well-crafted theoretical fiction by the advocates of a Muslim polity empowered them to choose an idiom within which they could arbitrarily remove the distinction between religion and politics in order to produce "a certain kind of polity" (89).

Prior to the partition of India in 1947 into two separate nation-states, a group of Western-educated Indian Muslims who constituted the Muslim League, the pivotal Muslim political organization in undivided India, ardently advocated the logic of creating a separate homeland for Indian Muslims. These Muslim leaders identified with the proclamation of a nation-state for Muslims that was put forth in 1930 by an illustrious poet, Sir Mohammed Iqbal (88). As Sara Suleri writes in her memoir, *Meatless Days*, "[T]he logic of arguing for independence unleashed odd thoughts in India, so that in 1930 the poet Iqbal's Allahabad Address to the Muslim League could contain visionary references to the idea of a separate Indian Muslim nation" (114). Sir Mohammad Iqbal propagated the theoretical construct of "Pakistan," prior to its creation. The British orchestrated the partition of India in 1947. The aftermath of this historical catastrophe was a traumatic dislocation of agrarian society in the villages as well as of the population in urban areas, "[who] one day awoke to find they no longer inhabited familiar homes but that most modern thing, a Hindu or a Muslim nation" (Suleri 116).

The civil war in 1971 saw a further division of Pakistan and the creation of another geographical space: Bangladesh. After the gruesome partition of India in 1947, which caused an indeterminacy in the concept of "nation," the establishment of Bangladesh as a nation-state created yet another indeterminacy. The aftermath of 1971 was a period of political instability in Pakistan. The country witnessed a series of coup d'e'tats, which were orchestrated by the army in order to install military dictatorships. Ironically, by dividing and redividing the Indian nation, the ardent nationalism of that era sought the cohesive structure of an entrenched and centralized nation-state.

Naipaul is critical of Pakistan as an Islamic republic because he is painfully aware of the country's political and economic fiascos and aware, as well, of the fundamentalist strategies adopted by the military regimes that have called the shots in this nation. John Cole pointed out that the 1980s economy of Pakistan was with a pitiful annual gross national product per inhabitant (88). Cole observed that the technological development of Pakistan was mediocre even compared to that of Iran (89). As Naipaul explains, an unbridgeable schism separates the two Muslim nations: "here desert was desert. Iran, with a population of thirty-five million, earned seventy-million dollars a day from its oil; Pakistan with twice the population, earned one hundred forty million dollars a month from its exports of rice, leather, and cotton" (86). Pakistan's economic structure encourages the transnational reincorporation of migrants into the nation-state. The dire straits that Pakistan finds itself in has led to the mushrooming of "manpower-export experts" who "studied the world's immigration laws and competitively gambled with their emigrant battalions," in order to determine what kind of workers could be sent to the nations of the First World (101). Naipaul draws the inference that "the state that had appeared to some as God itself, a complete earthly reward for the faithful, lived not so much by its agricultural exports or by the proceeds of its minor, secondary industries, as by the export of its people" (100).

Despite the power of religious faith to cement a bond among peoples of various ethnicities in Pakistan, economic and social forces within the polity continue to foster divisions among ethnic groups. For instance, although Karachi is a metropolis in Pakistan inhabited by peoples of various ethnicities, the sentiments of one ethnic group, the Sindhi, supercede all others because of their numbers, political clout, and wealth. This division along ethnic lines was so vivid that "there was talk of detaching Karachi as a federal district from the province of Sind" (100).[2] Naipaul tells the reader that religious faith had the power to cement a bond among peoples of various ethnicities in Pakistan, but that this bond was ephemeral because it lacked the simultaneous development of substantive institutions. According to Timothy F. Weiss, Naipaul attributes Pakistan's political failure to its unrelenting reliance on Islam (152). But I argue that the social and political mayhem in Pakistan could be attributed to the lack of political unity among the people of that country. Islam is the only common and fragile thread that links peoples of various ethnicities and languages to one another. Beyond that, the differences among the ethno-linguistic groups in Pakistan, the Pathans, the Punjabis, the Sindhis, the Baluchis, the Mohajirs, and the Bengalis, render the country a house divided against itself.

Naipaul argues that in order to create an alternative discourse as well as alternative epistemological structures, fundamentalist ideology in Pakistan created a myth of a seemingly all-encompassing religious unity that nullified the glaring historical differences among the ethno-linguistic groups and social castes in the country (152). Yet the author ignores the strategic maneuvers employed by the fundamentalists in that region to determine values that became axiomatic in Pakistani society. For instance, impassioned appeals of the clergy to the outdated concept of Islam bred rancorous hate against the former imperialist occupiers of the Muslim world and exploited the pitiful poverty and illiteracy of the majority of Muslims in the Indian subcontinent, who were unable to study the progressive concepts of the religion for themselves. This strategy of fortifying fundamentalism created a gulf between the "believers" and the "non-believers" rooted in contemporary politics, not ancient history. The ideology that was propounded by the ruling fundamentalist order since the creation of Pakistan reflected and reproduced the interests of the mullahcracy. The mullahs justified repression of the poor and dispossessed classes, subjugation of women, and honor killings with the language of culture and religion. Such practices led to the regrettable rupture of the Indian subcontinent and to a denial of science, technology, and historical understanding of the precepts of Islam. Naipaul notes that "history—which begins as a 'pleasant story of conquest'—becomes hopelessly confusing. And out of this more-than-colonial confusion some Pakistanis fabricated personalities for themselves, in which they were Islamic and conquerors and—in Pakistan—a little like people in exile from their glory. They become Turks or Moghuls. Or Arabs" (142). Said's notion of the discourse of power seems applicable to the situation described by Naipaul: "All human activity depends on controlling a radically unstable reality to which words approximate only by will or convention" (*Culture* 29). That is not to say, though, that all orders of will or convention are equivalent; Said, like Naipaul, was among those who criticized the kind of nationalist logic that was instituted in Pakistan, in which an image of the outer boundaries of the non-Islamic world as chaotic valorized the dominance of the fundamentalist order.

Moreover, Naipaul's description of Islamization in Pakistan is frighteningly similar to Edward Said's depiction of Orientalism in the Middle East (*Orientalism* 5). Said asserts that the premise of the subjugation of the Arab natives by the European colonizer was based on a fabulated representation of the world, which the colonial power concocted to dominate the imaginations and lives of the colonized. This enabled the dominant power to appropriate the East in order to diminish the threat it posed to European civilization. Similarly, Naipaul claims that the fundamentalists' desire to create a theological city-state would never be realized because it would require a negation of thought, a conjuring of images, and a re-etching of boundaries that would serve fundamentalist beliefs (142).

In making this argument, Naipaul conveniently glosses over the poet Iqbal's hope that an Indian Muslim state would foreground an Islam that would be rid of "the stamp that Arab imperialism was forced to give it" (142). Iqbal had argued for a rational Islam; he had sought to reconcile Islamic teachings and democracy, and in order to do so had tried to make the Qur'an speak to modern minds. Iqbal's endeavor was to bring about a reformation of a religion of law so that it could be perpetuated in a modern age as a liberal force. He tried to combine the concept of an Islamic state with the principles of a socialist state, advocating social equality and economic and political democratization. In order to do so, Iqbal endeavored to formulate a detailed logic and methodology that uses traditional interpretations of the Qur'an and traditional jurisprudential and legal issues to carve a new direction in Islamic thought (Smith 87). It is a terrible irony that an intellectual who labels the ferocity of the Ram Janmabhoomi movement, orchestrated in India by the Bharatiya Janata Party, "an awakening of history" should ignore the work of intellectuals like Iqbal.

A good corrective to Naipaul's views in this regard are those of Gayatri Spivak. Spivak speaks of postcolonial claims to nationhood, democracy, and economic justice as a form of "catachresis." The traditional definition of catachresis is the misapplication of a word or phrase, as in the case of a mixed metaphor. Spivak adapts this term to her argument by defining "catachresis" as "an effect produced by the displacement of European concept-metaphors from their proper context,"

> A [. . .] local, tactical maneuver, which involves wrenching particular images, ideas or rhetorical strategies out of their place within a particular narrative and using them to open up new arenas of meaning, often in direct contrast to their conventionally understood meanings and functions. (Spivak 234)

According to Spivak, the "construction" of the sovereign subject could be classified as "catachresis" in a transnational world in which identity rests upon a fragmented subjectivity that is dispersed over several dominant and peripheral practices rather than existing as a homogeneous and monologic entity. Spivak posits a postmodern/poststructuralist notion of nationalist identity as opposed to the dogmatic essentialism of the sense of identity promulgated by the mullahcracy.

The strategic use of this device can enable the process of displacement of theocratic discourse in the narrative of a state, such as Pakistan, which facilitates the assigning of "canonical" values to itself by drawing a homology between the religious ideal of Islam and the social order that it creates. Naipaul does not deploy a catachrestic concept of Islam in his travelogue. Instead, he uses the concept-metaphors that ratify the stereotypical image of the religion. For instance, he writes disparagingly about the zealous religious activities of the Ahmadis, an Islamic sect with which he gets acquainted while in Pakistan. While Naipaul does write about their attempts to propagate Islam in Africa by circulating Korans in Luganda, Swahili, and Yoruba, he does not underline the inevitable dialectical interplay between an antiquated Islam that was founded in Arabia and various indigenous cultures. This contiguity among disparate histories and races can and often has engendered a pluralistic vision of the world, not the fixity of a glorified vision of the past that the author finds inherent in the rhetoric of Islamic fundamentalism. Naipaul isn't wrong to see fundamentalism as a historical outcome of this commingling, but his vision is lopsided because he sees it as the most historically important outcome.

Naipaul continues to explore Islamic fundamentalism in relation to the dissemination of myths of an idyllic indigenous past in the third section of his travelogue, "Conversations in Malaysia: The Primitive Faith." Naipaul begins by writing about Joseph Conrad's portrayal of the "remoter places of the Malay Archipelago a hundred years ago," which ascribed a mystique to the native population and echoed the attempt of the colonial power to create a dichotomy between the European colonized and the Malay colonized (226). The confluence of the East and the West became one of Conrad's predominant themes: "Separate, colliding worlds: the world of Europeans, pushing on to the 'outer edge of darkness,' the closed tribal world of Malays" (226). But in today's Malaysia with its mélange of European, Arab, Chinese, and Malay peoples, transnational corporations and their invasion into insular rural existences have replaced the semi-mythical primitive land of rattan and coconut.

The country's attractiveness to transnational corporations has opened up the old ways of its forest and river civilization to subsequent material and cultural change. The myth of the immutability of tradition is proven fallacious. In his study of developing countries, Cole pointed out that compared to other developing countries, Malaysia has become moderately rich, with a higher gross national product per inhabitant than that of Pakistan and Iran (88–90). The accompanying irrevocable changes in terms of "money, development, education" in the country have caused a sense of frustration and hopelessness in the Malay villagers, who find their ventures stymied at every step. Naipaul writes:

> The old colonial town of Kuala Lumpur, the Malaysian capital, still survives in parts. Old tile-roofed private dwellings, originally British; the rows of narrow two-story Chinese shop-houses, the shops downstairs, the pavement pillared, the pavements supporting the projecting upper storey. . . .
>
> That colonial town has been left behind by the new residential developments, the skyscrapers of the new city, the Korean-built highways that lead in and from the airport, first through plantations . . . , and then

past the factories and the assembly plants of international companies. (228–29)

The disintegration of an agrarian economy and its concomitant social structure is verbalized for the author by a young student, Shafi. Shafi tells Naipaul of a batik factory by the Chinese community that befouled a stream near his native village. An embittered Shafi tells the author the contamination of the stream "disturbed our swimming activities in the small stream nearby. They spoilt our playground" (293).

Through the superceding of a pre-capitalist economy by a capitalist one, the country has been subjected to nationalizing and transnationalizing trends simultaneously. This foray of transnational practices into a national territory creates a profound contradiction within rural communities. Not only is the social organization of rural communities rendered inadequate, but the political and economic bases for the material and cultural connections within these communities are corroded.

The processes of "forest exploitation, mineral extraction, a concentration on cash crops, and a stimulated consumerism" have widened the gap between the industrial society in urban areas and the agrarian one in the remote regions of the country, ravaging local forms of subsistence and cottage-industry production. The penetration of transnational capital and investments into the local economy increases the dependence of the country on the First World. Naipaul tells us, "Money magnified the limitations of places like Malaysia, small, uneducated, and coming late to everything. Money . . . changed old ways. But money only turned people into buyers of imported goods, fixed the country in a dependent relationship with the developed world, kept all men colonials" (266).

This incursion of transnationalism into former hinterlands greatly increases the spread of culturally focused revolutionary movements, like the movements of Islamic fundamentalism in Malaysia, Pakistan, Iran, Egypt, and Nigeria. The Islamic revival in Malaysia, which Naipaul designates the Malay "way of getting even with the world," is the corollary to the tensions generated by the new set of relations between the First World and the Third World. In the transnational context, the insularity of the Third-World bourgeoisie and the rabidity of the havoc it wreaks on the agrarian social relations in its country of origin leaves the native working class and petty bourgeoisie with recourse to the abstractions of faith and a fantastic hope in the recreation of an earthly paradise. As George Simmel noted long ago, the increased division of labor that was caused by industrialization undermines the older organization of society, which was founded on kinship, cultural, and caste affiliations (275). In other words, the transformations that occurred with urbanization could not be reconciled with traditional and rural communities. As Naipaul tells us about the effects of commercialized economy on the Malay villager, Shafi "felt that as a Malay he had nothing; and in reaction he wished—as though such a thing was possible—to be nothing but his faith, a kind of abstract man" (292).

Naipaul finds a similar revival of Islamic fundamentalist forces in Indonesia. Like Malaysia, neighboring Indonesia had experienced social upheaval, war, and revolution in the twentieth century. In 1965, a military coup dislodged the regime of President Sukarno, and the consequence was the chaotic mushrooming of insurgencies all over the country as well as the massacre of Chinese and individuals alleged of being communist supporters. Naipaul writes, "There was a massacre of Chinese (resident in Indonesia for centuries, and traditional victims of pogroms: the Dutch themselves killed many thousands in Jakarta in 1740). And it is said that in popular uprisings all over the archipelago half a million people thought to be communists were hunted down and killed. Some people say a million" (299). The devastation in the wake of the organized pogrom created a regressive nostalgia for the unsullied innocence of a mythical past. The rapid urbanization of Indonesia and the foray of transnational practices into its sphere were responsible for the intensification of the fierceness of culturally rooted movements, such as Islam. Fundamentalist Islam provides a framework within which the fantasy of the return to a simpler past can be nurtured: it "makes people withdraw, the more violently to leap forward" (300).

But in postcolonial societies, the challenge lies in being able to leave "part of the past behind, in working through it to imagine agency and self-hood in positive terms, inventing new dimensions of cultural possibility" (Mohanty 288). In the literature on transnationalism, there remains a tension between postmodern theories of understanding the power differential that sustains positions of power and privilege and an identity "imbedded" in collectivities and collective action. As Luis Eduardo Guarnizo and Michael Peter Smith put it:

> There is a tension in the literature on transnationalism between postmodern cultural studies' conception of identity construction as a free-floating, if not voluntaristic, process of individual self-formation and the many empirical studies of bi-national migrants, transnational social movements, and international organizational networks which envisage personal identity as embedded in socially structured and politically mediated processes of group formation and collective action. (20)

This tension is generated because transnational groups proudly profess loyalty to their ethno-national origins and contribute culturally and economically not just to their host societies, but to their homelands as well.

At the same time, transnational groups have been affected by the processes of globalization, nationalism, regionalization, international migration, and religious fundamentalism. These new trends are in strong contrast to the earlier political and social aspects of ethno-nationalism, as noted by Naipaul in his earlier fiction. For instance, in one work he states,

> Nationalism was impossible in Trinidad. In the colonial society every man had to be for himself; every man had to grasp whatever dignity and power he was allowed; he owned no loyalty to the island and scarcely any to his group. (*The Middle Passage* 65)

This sort of behavior, Naipaul implies, is owing to caste and race barriers as well as to a dearth of significant indigenous institutions and thought systems.

The inability to transcend caste and race barriers in post-colonial Trinidad renders the colonial subject incapable of forging a nationalistic solidarity in the community. This blatant failure enables Naipaul to present the colonial politician, Ganesh, as an "easy object of satire" (*The Mimic Men* 208). Naipaul paints Ganesh in an even more risible light in *The Mystic Masseur*. Ganesh is portrayed as an ambitious man who is able to make headway by shunning loyalties and responsibilities. In trying to establish himself as a successful man, Ganesh assumes several identities in succession: teacher, masseur, mystic, and member of the legislative council. Despite his dexterity in various public roles, however, Ganesh is unable to don the mantle of a selfless political leader. Similarly, the ambitious politician in the village of Elvira, Harbans, is unable to assist in the evolution of democracy as a form of government in which the interests of every socio-economic class are taken into consideration. Patrick Johnson finds in Naipaul an obsequious willingness to "serve up a view of Third World politics palatable only to a colonialist sensibility" (14).

The feeling of despondency that Naipaul depicts as the inevitable consequence of living in a colonial backwater is vividly portrayed in *A House for Mr. Biswas*. The protagonist of the novel, Mohun Biswas, is the descendant of an Indian laborer who was indentured to Trinidad. The deracinating forces of colonialism and dislocation had caused Biswas's cultural heritage to disintegrate. He is, therefore, burdened with the task of re-creating his Indian cultural heritage in an alien land. Murray S. Martin concludes that Naipaul's work is "affected by the history of his own island home and by its

place in the world scheme of things" (33). Naipaul represents Biswas as alien-
ated and dejected because in order to re-create Indian traditions and rituals
in a West Indian colony, the protagonist willfully has to ignore socially structured and politically mediated processes of group formation. In other words,
Biswas's conception of the nation is an idealized and holistic version of how
it might be, ignoring the attempts of various transnational movements to
transgress the boundaries of the nation and reach out beyond them.[3]

The example of Naipaul's Mr. Biswas suggests that transnationalism
may be unable to vanquish the overwhelming power of both Western and
Eastern institutions—in other words, may be unable to construct and reconstruct identities. This view would oppose Homi Bhabha's theorization of
hybrid, transnational subjectivities as constituting "counter-narratives of the
nation" that subvert nationalist identities. According to Bhabha, the site of
ambivalence created by transnational identities and practices is the spaces in
which a "hybrid" identity emerges. The "hybrid" identity created in this contradictory space annuls the hierarchical purity of cultures. This notion of
hybridity, as theorized by Bhabha, challenges the inequality between various
cultural, linguistic, and political valences. This term is meant to suggest a
leveling of oppositions that generates "interstices," which in turn constitute
the terrain for the displacement of clearly defined boundaries. These interstitial passages which open up small and narrow fissures between seemingly
intransigent identities supposedly create the possibility of the blossoming of
cultural hybridities that undermine hierarchical structures (4).

Bhabha contends that the concept of homogeneity in national cultures
and in communities defined by their ethnicity is in the process of being redefined (5). But transnational subjects seek to recapture a lost sense of belonging by underlining cultural and political connections to the nation of origin.
These identities forged by transnational subjects are not inherently counter-
hegemonic, but can create as essentialized an area of social and cultural
knowledge as that created by nation-states. For instance, the protagonist of *A
House for Mr. Biswas* constantly strives to achieve a sense of the past, his cultural history, and his ancestral home. Biswas's rekindling of the past imposes
an obtrusive pattern on his life and stymies him from making a foray into
the world of urbanity and social change.

In other words, the identity imposed on a subject by transnational discourses can deny the power of choice to those at the margins of society, those
whose cultural identity has been dislocated: migrants in ghettoized edges of
the city, who live hand to mouth in the first world for a better life while
struggling at the lowest levels of those societies. But in order to propose alternative accounts of the nation, one would need to think of the postcolonial

nation in terms of those people who exist at the margins of society. Resistance movements that have been interwoven by transnational links have had the most powerful impact in the twentieth century.

The transnational realm within which such movements blossom entails the assertion of an identity that does not lose a sense of history and context, but at the same time, points out the necessary caution that our cultural identities and the social and political knowledge that they provide us access to, are never essentialized, but historically open-ended (Mohanty 232). In other words, the re-membering of cultural identities should be propounded as an attempt to challenge the Western and Eastern institutionalization of patriarchal national imperialisms in order to delegitimize a narrative that attempts to homogenize national identity. This form of inquiry would traverse various social spaces, such as translocal migrant networks, transnational social groups (e.g., International Alliance of Women, Development Alternatives with Women for a New Era, Women Living Under Muslim Laws International Solidarity Network, etc.), and globalized liberal state ideology (democracy, liberty, free enterprise capitalism), as affecting the formation of identity:

> Through these networks, an increasing number of people are able to live dual lives. Participants are often bilingual, move easily between different cultures, frequently maintain homes in two countries, and pursue economic, political and cultural interests that require their presence in both. (Conner 8)

Identity fluctuates as the spaces through which people move change, enabling the reader to interpret the world through specific identities of history, culture, traditional links to land without the simplification that cultural relativism or postmodernism entail:

> Personal identity formation in transnational social spaces can best be understood as a dialectic of embedding and disembodying which, over time, involves an unavoidable encumbering, dis-encumbering, and re-encumbering of situated selves. Identity is contextual but not radically discontinuous. People seek to be situated, to have a stable mooring, an anchor amidst the tempest. (Guarnizo and Smith 21)

Cultures and societies not only represent and perpetuate values, but can also provide empirical reasoning to create alternative, socially structured bases. While the complexities bred by transnational cultural, political, and economic practices and identities can reinforce a nationalist agenda and can lead to the fanatical espousal of tradition, transnational also has positive effects,

which have been celebrated in terms such as *hybridity* and celebratory multiculturalism, my argument suggests why these sort of terms, too, cannot be a
stopping-place for our thinking about a world radically transformed by postcolonial struggles.

Chapter Three

Transnationalism as Hybridization in Rushdie's *The Satanic Verses*

The Satanic Verses is not, in my view, an antireligious novel. It is an attempt to write about migration, its stresses and transformations, from the point of view of migrants from the subcontinent to Britain. This, for me, is the saddest irony of all; that after working for five years to give voice and fictional flesh to the immigrant culture of which I myself am a member, I should see my book burned, largely unread by the people it's about. I tried to write about stereotypes; the zealot protests serve to confirm, in the Western mind, all the worst stereotypes of the Muslim world. (Rushdie qtd. in Mariani 96)

As everyone knows, Salman Rushdie's *The Satanic Verses* caused an upheaval in the Islamic world. The furor surrounding the book incited the Iranian Shiite religious leader, Ayatollah Khomeini, to issue an edict demanding the author's head on a platter. Because of the jeopardy his life was in, Rushdie went in hiding from 1989 until 2001. The decision to ban the book was taken by some countries in order to quell the unrest caused by the vociferous protests of national and transnational Muslim communities against the ostensibly blasphemous "Mahound" and "Ayesha" sections (Pipes 112). Important literary and political issues arose from this affair.

In order to grasp the significance of his involvement in these issues, some knowledge of Rushdie's other writings is required. Rushdie's oeuvre attempts to revive the genre of myth in order to formulate a "viable alternative ideology" to the deadlock of Manichean binaries that confronts the subject in postcolonial societies (Afzal-Khan 173). These binaries accentuated by former colonial regimes include black and white, savage and civilized, silent and articulate, rational ruler and irrational ruled. Rushdie's novels are embodiments of his rejection of subject-object dialectic. As in *Grimus, Midnight's*

Children, Shame, and *The Satanic Verses,* the author deploys the genre of myth in order to create a postmodern metafiction that melds fiction and history, the magical and the real. Like the protagonists of Rushdie's earlier works, the protagonists of *The Satanic Verses* embody identity as a constantly shifting and fluid experience. In addition to eroding the idea of determinant concepts, univocal meanings, and recoverable origins, the conventions of historical time get subverted in these narratives.

Rushdie foregrounds the social, political, and religious framework created by Mahound in order to underscore the asphyxiation caused by the institutionalized authority of the Islamic East that culls the details of the life of the Prophet Mohammad that Islamic jurisprudence sets as precedents governing every aspect of a Muslim's life. Referring to the Prophet Mohammad as "Mahound," in this context, suggests that institutionalized Islam's prophet is not, in fact, the real one but rather a viciously purified stereotype of "pristineness."

In accordance with his consistent practice of challenging dichotomies or "Manichean binaries," Rushdie effectively eliminates the polarized distinction between the sacred and the profane. In this chapter, I argue that Rushdie's fiction is complex because of the "chutnification" of Western and Eastern forms, the mixture of myth and reality, of genres, of media and languages. The metaphor of "chutnification" refers to the traditional Indian condiment that combines various ingredients, such as basil, mint, coriander, tamarind, turmeric, and peppers. This image is designed to suggest the amalgamation of the past, present, and future that would lead to the transmutation of the brutality of history into more palatable versions.

As I mentioned earlier, Rushdie's narratives are postmodern metafictions. Patricia Waugh defines this mode of writing as, "fictional writing which self-consciously and systematically draws attention to itself as an artifact to pose questions about the relationship between fiction and reality" (59). Rushdie's metafictional narratives make an overt use of fabulation so as to foreground the constant potential for a fiction to take off from history. In these narratives, fabulation entails the employment of the literary device, pastiche. The concept of pastiche refers to the imitation of various styles without the comic absurdity that one finds in parody. According to Fredric Jameson, in the postmodern age of fragmentation and unstable points of reference, parody has been relegated to the background and pastiche has taken its place (56). The self-reflexivity of these novels problematizes the issue of historical knowledge and of a national identity. Commenting on the ludicrousness of a search for an uncontaminated national identity in a transnational era, Rushdie says:

> One of the most absurd aspects of this quest for national authenticity is
> that it is completely fallacious to suppose that there is such a thing as
> pure, unalloyed tradition from which to draw. The only people who
> seriously believe this are religious fanatics. (*Imaginary Homelands* 67)

Timothy Brennan develops a critique of the severance of Third-World writers like Rushdie from the myth of nationalism. According to Brennan, the
attitude of such "cosmopolitan writers of the Third World" toward a national
myth exhibits a "creative duplicity." With these writers, Brennan contends,
the literary devices of "allusion, metaphor, allegorical parable are all like
nationalism itself, 'janus-faced,' with one face toward the West" (30–1).[1] He
advocates "impassioned sarcasm" as "the appropriate stylistic elements for
historical-political action," in place of Rushdie's pastiche (135).

   Similarly, Aijaz Ahmad critiques Rushdie's inability to engage responsi-
bly with issues of historical and political importance in Third World nations:
". . . so wedded is Rushdie's imagination to imageries of wholesale degradation and unrelieved social wreckage, so little is he able to conceive of a real
possibility of regenerative projects on the part of those who actually exist
within our contemporary social reality . . ." (149–50). For Tim Parnell like-
wise, by straddling the "boundaries between the fictional and the historical"
Rushdie's novels reflect the "labyrinth cunningly constructed by an imperial
past," thereby denying the people of the Indian subcontinent any possibility
of eluding it. (255)

   It is worth noting that some critics counter the above criticisms of
Rushdie's oeuvre by reading his novels disinterestedly. For instance, Malise
Ruthven notes that *The Satanic Verses* "contains an ambivalence" that sets it
up as "a kind of anti-Qur'an which challenges the original by substituting for
the latter's absolutist certainties a theology of doubt" (16). In other words,
Rushdie's work represents a formidable challenge to oppressive authority.
This position is elucidated by Anuradha Dingwaney Needham: "We do not
find a unitary, monolithic identity in Rushdie; rather his work reflects a conception of post-colonial identity that is fluid, multiple, shifting, and responsive to varied situations and varied audiences" (149). I would point out that
this fluidity of meaning in Rushdie's work is exemplified in his prose style, in
which meaning is contingent on the "bastardization" of the English language
rather than on the structures inherent in the language.

   Rushdie's first novel, *Grimus* (1975), for instance, is a mélange of
myth, fantasy, and science fiction. Myth and magic in this novel are made to
suggest the fusing of the genres of the real and the unreal as a "strategy of liberation." Rushdie attempts to navigate through these alternating political

and religious understandings of the world in more radical terms in *Midnight's Children* (1981). The novel is an allegorical rendition of the history of modern India. The narrator, Saleem Sinai's, psyche is wrenched by a personal history that parallels the traumas and tribulations of an independent India. Having witnessed the two Indo-Pakistan wars of 1965 and 1971 and having seen their horrendous effects, he consciously withdraws from history by developing selective amnesia. He looks for solace in the pickle factory where he is employed and strives to achieve the "chutnification" or transmutation of history into a safe haven, away from the distresses of the real world: "Every pickle-jar contains the most exalted of possibilities: the feasibility of the chutnification of history; the grand hope of the pickling of time!" (Rushdie, *Children* 548).[2] As in *Grimus,* myth and magic in this novel are made to suggest the fusing of the genres of the real and the surreal as a "strategy of liberation."

In his third novel, *Shame* (1983), Rushdie again deploys the metaphor of the "chutnification" of history to suggest the amalgamation of the past, present, and future. As in *Grimus* and *Midnight's Children,* Rushdie deploys the genre of myth in order to meld or "chutnify" fiction and history, the magical and the real.

In *The Satanic Verses* (1988), Rushdie again challenges generic and ideological constructions that fabricate deleterious dichotomous structures. I analyze his fictive strategies in the rest of this chapter. I look at the ramifications of Westernization and the role of religion and politics in the postcolonial nation-state. The postmodernist structure of *The Satanic Verses* with its complex fusion of ideas, personal and national identity, the relationship between good and evil, the nature of the matrix within which we live, generate a highly complex fictional topography. As Rushdie admits:

> *The Satanic Verses* is very big. There are certain of architecture that are dispensed with. *Midnight's Children* had history as a scaffolding on which to hang the book; this one doesn't. And since it's so much about transformation I wanted to write it in such a way that the book itself was metamorphosing all the time. Obviously the danger is the book falls apart. (qtd. in Appignanesi and Maitland 6–7).

As Pierre François observes, this novel about fragmentation and reintegration is divided into odd-and-even-numbered sections. The first four of the odd sections, I to VII take place in London, while the last, IX, is set in Bombay. Section II ("Mahound") relates the story of the original revelation to the prophet of Islam, including the "satanic verses" episode; section IV, ("Ayesha") tells the story of the Imam who is the caricature of Ayatollah

Khomeini, before going on to tell the story of the girl Ayesha, who proposes a pilgrimage from Pakistan to Mecca by walking into the Arabian Sea; section VI, ("Return to Jahilia") relates the story of the spread and establishment of Islam, and the fortification of the monolithic "Idea," including Baal's defiance of that idea; section VII, ("The Parting of the Arabian Sea") recapitulates the fallout of Ayesha's pilgrimage.

The narrative of *The Satanic Verses* is self-conscious, narcissistic, introspective, and auto-representational. As a strategy to employ intertextual references and allusions by examining historical and fictional systems, the author puts himself into the postmodern metanarrative by intruding to comment and involving himself with the fictional characters. As Rushdie says, "I do not believe that novels are trivial matters. The ones I care most about are those which attempt radical reformulations of language, form, and ideas, those that attempt to do what the word novel seems to insist upon: to see the world anew" (*Imaginary Homelands* 314).

These issues are all relevant to one of the novel's protagonists, Gibreel Farishta, who belongs to the deified class of Indian movie stars. He is a famous and flamboyant Bombay superstar, portraying the pantheon of Hindu deities of the Indian subcontinent in movies with religious themes. Gibreel, however, faces a dilemma. After he lands in London, he feels caught between two irreconcilable worlds. He struggles between a mythologized and "pristine" cultural past, as represented in the religious movies, and the disjointed and dislocated present of the immigrant with its "chutnified" culture. So, as an actor, Gibreel attempts to negotiate the space between the world of reality, represented by his vulnerable mortal state, and the world of dreams, represented by the deities whom he portrays in the movies. Thus, Gibreel's identity is constantly deconstructed and reconstructed in the "in-between" spaces of the world of dreams and the world of reality, between the world of anthropomorphized deities and that of puny mortals. As Sara Suleri succinctly points out, the name "Gibreel Farishta" translates as "Gabriel Angel," "hardly the most appropriate name for an actor most renowned for his cinematic portrayals of Hindu deities" ("Contraband" 612). Gibreel is portrayed as an embodiment of the Archangel Gabriel, who dictates the word of God to the prophet Mohammad and dreams the world of the magical narratives in the novel: "Gibreel was sweating with fear: 'every time I go to sleep the dream starts up from where it stopped. Same dream in the same place. As if somebody just paused the video while I went out of the room. Or, or. As if he's the guy who's awake and this is the bloody nightmare. His bloody dream: us. Here. All of it'" (83). These dreams begin after Gibreel and the other protagonist of the novel, Saladin Chamcha, are held hostage on an Air

India jet that is hijacked to London, and Gibreel reads a pamphlet about creationism that propagates the notion of a supreme entity controlling the universe.

During his dreams, Gibreel, in his embodiment of the Angel Gabriel, sees himself revealing divine messages to the prophet of Islam, referred to by the derogatory medieval term of "Mahound" in the novel. At times, he is unable to draw a line of demarcation between himself and Mahound. This blurring of distinctions in his dreams evokes a sense of panic in Gibreel because he begins to question the integrity or cohesiveness of his own sense of being:

> . . . , and now Gibreel, who has been hovering-above-looking-down, feels a confusion, who am I, in these moments it begins to seem that the archangel is actually inside the prophet, I am dragging in the gut, I am the angel being extruded from the sleeper's navel, I emerge, Gibreel Farishta, while my other self, Mahound, lies listening, entranced, I am bound to him, navel by navel, by a shining cord of light, not possible to say which of us is dreaming the other. We flow in both directions along the umbilical cord. (110)

As Gibreel's embrace of the derogatory term "Mahound" indicates, these dreams create a realm within which questions of identity do not maintain a binary perspective that divides the world into pigeonholes such as reality versus fantasy or self versus other.

The resultant discourse leads to Gibreel identifying his " 'angel' self as another person: in the Beckettian formula, Not I. He" (350). The reader is constantly reminded of the inextricable "umbilical cord" that binds Gibreel to the prophet of Islam. The character possesses a second identity that is located in the past, but that has its point of departure in the present. Thus, in the words of Damian Grant, fiction gets imbricated with what "Beckett has most unremittingly analyzed as the migrant voice, migrant in an ultimate sense, that travels with its supply of words through all the categories of culture" (75). In other words, the attempt to create an identity or to reintegrate a fragmented identity is implicated within the diverse possibilities that fiction offers us.

The other protagonist, Saladin Chamcha, is an embodiment of the "mongrelization" of the immigrant. Ironically, given his name—Saladin was a legendary Muslim warrior—Chamcha uncritically adopts everything the British represent and detests his Indian past, represented by his father and the house in Bombay that reeks of his childhood memories. Like Gibreel, Saladin is involved in the entertainment business. As an actor, he is much in demand on radio and in television commercials: "Once in a radio play for thirty-seven voices, he interpreted every single part under a variety of pseudonyms and nobody ever worked it out" (60–61). In his professional life, Saladin is the ultimate dislocated immigrant, abjectly mimicking the cultural and social values, or "voices," of the colonizer. This is not to say, however, that he has easily acculturated himself to England and all that it represents. On the contrary, Rushdie takes pains to show us how much Saladin did not fit in at his English school. In one excruciatingly funny scene, we see Saladin Chamcha spend ninety minutes trying to eat a kipper at breakfast. Although the elusive kipper frustrates him, his peers remain passive observers and do not offer to mitigate the difficult task of dissecting this symbol of Englishness. It is at this point that Saladin resolves to establish himself as a full-fledged member of English society (44).[3] Saladin's success in conquering the elusive kipper is for his Indian palate an assertion of his anglicized taste and of the anglicized voices that come from it.

In the character of Saladin, Rushdie portrays the displaced migrant who, as he gnaws at a new culture, is gnawed at by the need to fit into the community of adoption. Like Saladin aspires to repudiate the subcontinental past epitomized by his domineering father, Changez Chamchawala. Saladin's assiduous efforts to get assimilated into British culture are underlined by his lack of sympathy with his native culture; in fact, they begin while he is still in Bombay: "When the England cricket team played India at the Brabourne Stadium, he prayed for an England victory, for the game's creators to defeat the local upstarts, for the proper order of things to be maintained" (37). For him, the civility, rationality, and fair-mindedness of the English are indubitable. In order to "fit in," Saladin emulates an Oxbridge accent as well as the mannerisms of the English. This metamorphosis entails a willing relinquishment of the past and of everything that it held sacred. Sabrina Hassumani sums up Saladin's espousal of "Englishness" as "a negative moment in the text," because Saladin Chamcha is unable to "incorporate 'India' into his new 'English' experience" (79). But I suggest that Saladin survives his painful metamorphosis because he returns to his roots while recognizing the nuances of the culture and political history of the phenomenon of migration, displacement, and life in a ghettoized group.

Prior to the flight back to London from Bombay on which he gets entangled with Gibreel, Saladin's lack of filiative and affiliative loyalty to the culture into which he was born is brought out vividly on his visit to a restaurant. He is taken to this restaurant by an old childhood acquaintance, Zeeny Vakil. Zeeny bluntly tells Saladin that he is a toady of the English and his constructed identity is responsible for his "slave mentality." Meanwhile, a cacophony is raised around them by the vociferous arguments within Zeeny's group of armchair politicians about the political turmoil on the subcontinent. Issues that Saladin has never had to confront or even consider are brought up in that polyvocal argument: radical and anti-colonial notions that hold the First World responsible for bamboozling the Third World, the extreme poverty that afflicts the Indian populace, and the facts of a reality pervaded by violence. This aggressive discussion nauseates Saladin: "He had to accept the fact that his blood no longer contained the immunizing agents that would have enabled him to suffer India's reality" (58).[4] His severance from India's reality eggs him on to launch an outrageous tirade against the culture and its representatives, which he denounces as irreparable and hopeless. Shortly after this event, when he falls ill, still in Bombay, the reality of his cultural transmogrification hits him, and he continues this tirade in his delirium: "I don't like people dropping in to see me without warning, I have forgotten the rules of seven-tiles and kabaddi, I can't recite my prayers, I don't know what would happen at a nikkah ceremony, and in this city where I grew up I get lost if I'm on my own. This isn't home" (58). He convinces himself that to go "home" after so long was a regression, and he continues to rant and rave about his social and cultural alienation.

Through this character, Rushdie suggests not only that the sacredness accorded to the notion of nationalism is problematic, but that the reality of exile and the inevitable sense of displacement that it generates is just as complex.[5]

The fact that Saladin chooses to ignore his Indian identity does not mean that it does not exist. Saladin's state of being is defined by the porousness of the lines of demarcation between an English identity and an Indian one.

The corollary of Saladin's complete assimilation into English culture would be an erasure of his Indian identity, which, as Rushdie suggests, is a pipe dream. For instance, during Saladin's trip to India, just before his eventful flight back to London, he dreams of a "bizarre stranger" who implores Saladin to release him from the stifling skin of glass within which he feels incarcerated. In his dream, Saladin cracks the glass and attempts to separate the shards of broken glass in the skin, but in the process he ends up removing pieces of flesh that cleave to the shards. Rushdie draws a thought-provoking parallel between this dream and the plight of the immigrant in a later scene in which Saladin's childhood acquaintance, Zeeny, remarks that she and her vociferous peers have been successful in cracking his anglicized shell. Saladin responds to this barb by saying, "Well this is what's inside. . . . An Indian translated into English-medium. . . . When you have stepped through the looking-glass you step at your peril. The mirror may cut you to shreds" (58). The man with the glass skin represents the immigrant who, despite his servile mimicry, remains empty and essentially invisible. He has no subjectivity of his own, and the glass shell that substitutes for a meaningful identity is liable to crack at any moment.

For instance, on his flight back from London to Bombay, he finds himself asking the in-flight attendant for a drink in a Bombay lilt: "Achha, means what? . . . So, okay, bibi, give one whiskey soda only" (34). "Achha" is an idiomatic term that means "okay" or "so." The term is usually used to express surprise or satisfaction. Of this foray of his accent into the putatively "impregnable" boundaries of his Englishness, Saladin thinks, "What a nasty surprise! He had come awake with a jolt, and sat stiffly in his chair. . . . How had the past bubbled up, in transmogrified vowels and vocab? What next? Would he take to putting coconut oil in his hair?" (34). Saladin's constructed identity then seems to be shattering even more when the plane that he is on is hijacked by terrorists and explodes in mid-air: "He was possessed by the nightmare fear of cracking, of seeing his blood bubbling up from the ice-breaks, of his flesh coming away from the shards" (131). Saladin's attempt to remove himself from the culture into which he was born turns out to be a fiasco because in order to achieve his end, Rushdie tells the reader, Saladin would need to "construct everything from scratch" (132).

The narrator draws a parallel between Saladin's endeavor to recreate himself and that of Satan to be his own lord and master. A migrant who attempts such a task is described as

> unnatural, a blasphemer, an abomination of abominations. From another angle, you could see pathos in him, heroism in his struggle, in his willingness to risk: not all mutants survive. Or, consider him sociopolitically: most migrants learn and can become disguises. Our own false descriptions to counter the falsehoods invented about us, concealing for reasons of security our secret selves. (49)

The migrant is described as a person who is capable of inventing himself by being a versatile mimic. In the case of Saladin, the migrant is an immaculate mimic of the voice of an Englishman, similar to the way Satan was an unerring mimic of the voice of Allah. Another similarity between the two is that the migrant attempts to appropriate the discourse of power in order to subvert it. In this attempt to recreate identity, however, unless the migrant is successful in creating a new transnational space, he or she risks either uncritical assimilation or monstrous reincarnation. For Saladin, neither uncritical anglicization nor a satanic degeneration is a viable alternative. Like the protagonists of Rushdie's earlier works, he embodies identity as a constantly shifting and fluid experience.

Saladin continues to be enmeshed in an ambivalent realm, while Gibreel is anxious about slippage between the two worlds: "the two men,

Gibreelsaladin Farishtachamcha condemned to their endless but also ending angel devilish fall" (5). In the "Ellowen Deeowen" section of the novel, Gibreel and Saladin land in England as the fortunate survivors of the hijacked Air India jet that is blown into smithereens by the hijackers. Saladin's metamorphosis leads the British police to accuse him of being an illegal immigrant. His transmogrification is treated by the police "as if it were the most banal and familiar matter they could imagine" (158). Meanwhile, Gibreel finds refuge in the care of Rosa Diamond, an eighty-eight year old woman, who is "the creature of cracks and absences she knew herself to be" (130). The sight of Gibreel Farishta invokes for Rosa Diamond memories of her late husband, Don Enrique Diamond, who was an agent of the colonial enterprise on the pampas in Argentina, mimicking the colonial ideologies of patriotism and patriarchy.

In her senility, she dwells on nostalgic longings for the life of opulence and luxury that she led with her husband on the pampas, and Gibreel identifies with this fantasy world: "Gibreel Farishta: felt her stories winding round him like a web, holding him in that lost world where fifty sat down to dinner every day, what men they were, our gauchos, nothing servile there, very fierce and proud" (150–51). So when Rosa Diamond tells him that he looks just like her late husband, he masquerades as Don Enrique, causing a breach between the historical continuum of past and present. His mimicry is successful because, as the narrator tells the reader, "it was not possible to distinguish memory from wishes, or guilty reconstructions from confessional truths" (157). Gibreel's masquerade as Don Enrique Diamond is another possibility offered by the fiction to reintegrate his fragmented identity. However, this possibility turns out to be unsatisfactory because it suggests the totalizing form of the discourse of Europe that depends on a dichotomy between the authorized notion of empire and the reality of the former colonized world.

Subsequent to the death of the octogenarian, Gibreel wends his way from Rosa's home to London. Along the way he is haunted by the fear that "God has decided to punish him for his loss of faith by driving him insane" or, in other words, by "the terror of losing his mind to a paradox, of being unmade by what he no longer believed existed, of turning in his madness into the avatar of a chimerical archangel"—that is, the archangel Gabriel (189). Gibreel's unregulated emotions open the floodgates of his mind and give way to a catastrophic deluge when he has a lurid vision of God: "and as the spirits of the world of dreams flooded through the breach into the universe of the quotidian, Gibreel Farishta saw God" (318). In the uproarious passage that follows, the reader is told that Gibreel's vision is of the "myopic scrivener" Salman Rushdie himself: "the apparition was balding, seemed to suffer from dandruff and wore glasses" (318). Gibreel's terror wraps him in a delusionary atmosphere in which his ambition is to replace the author-God by adopting a stance of rigidity, a stance very unlike that of Rushdie, who thrives on ambiguity. The paradox that Gibreel seeks to do away with is "Whether We be multiform, plural, representing the union-by-hybridiation . . . , or whether We be pure, stark, extreme . . ." (319). As he does in *Midnight's Children*, Rushdie attempts to highlight plurality as opposed to purity. Gibreel's fantasies, however, make a foray into the real world and submerge his identity. He sees a rupture occurring "not in him, but in the universe"; there are now "two realities, this world and another that was also right there, visible but unseen" (Rushdie, *Verses* 347). The cleavage in the universe becomes clear when Gibreel realizes that it is his voice that tempts Mahound into accepting the "satanic verses" that would compromise Islam into recognizing the hallowed status of the three goddesses Al-Lat, Manat, and Uzza: "it was me both times, baba, me first and second also me. From my mouth, both the statement and the repudiation, verses and converses, universes and reverses, the whole thing, and we all know how my mouth got worked" (123). Unable to reconcile to the notion of himself as the Archangel Gabriel, who encompasses good as well as evil, Gabriel is frightened by the idea of "chutnification," be it religious or cultural.

At one point, he turns on the author-God and demands to know what the origin of the words he spouts is, because they are "not his; never his original material. Then whose? He can't work it out" (234). Abandoning such questions and complexities, he finds solace in uncomplicated dichotomous versions of the universe, allowing him to construct a light Gabriel (Gibreel)/dark Satan (Shaitan) binary:

> No more of these England-induced ambiguities, these Biblical-Satanic confusions! Forget those son-of-the-morning fictions. . . . How much more straightforward this version was! How much more practical, down-to-earth, comprehensible!—Iblis/Shaitan standing for the darkness, Gibreel for the light.—Out, out with these sentimentalities: joining, locking together, love. Seek and destroy: that was all. (351–3)

Armed with this attitude, Gibreel sets out to save London from itself, but to his horror he discovers that the city refuses to yield to the arbitrary boundaries and distinctions drawn by cartographers. In his disintegrating vision, London is manifested as a heterogeneous mélange of places, cultures, and languages that recalls the "impure" works of Bertolt Brecht and Jean Luc Godard, *Mahagonny* and *Alphaville*, respectively: "This is no Proper London:

not this improper city. Airstrip One, Mahagonny, Alphaville. He wanders through a confusion of languages" (459). In this mosaic of a city, still subscribing to his fantastic notion of an ideally homogeneous self, Gibreel can save himself only by committing suicide. Whereas Saladin is rendered capable of embracing an eclecticism represented by Zeeny and her group of friends, which includes poets, filmmakers, journalists, and political activists, Gibreel fails because he is unable to form a composite identity.

How did the opposing fates of these two characters come to be yoked together? The narrative of *The Satanic Verses* begins with the fall of the two protagonists from a hijacked plane while flying over London. The plane blows into smithereens after it is bombed by terrorists. In their fall, the two protagonists embrace each other, and in this entanglement their identities merge:

> For whatever reason, the two men, Gibreelsaladin Farishtachamcha, condemned to endless but also ending angelic devilish fall, did not become aware of the moment at which the processes of their transmutation began. (5)

The transmutation is Rushdie's device for suggesting that Gibreel Farishta and Saladin Chamcha are entangled in a series of racial and political complexities. The "twin" protagonists of the book undergo a reciprocal metamorphosis during which Gibreel acquires a halo and Saladin sprouts demonic horns, hair, and hooves. However, this transmogrification does not enable the reader to draw a clear line of demarcation between two polarized identities. In the intertwining of the two protagonists during the course of their fall from the heavens, internal and external divisions within the immigrant community are rendered fuzzy. The angel and devil represented by Gibreel and Saladin, respectively, do not exist as separate entities, but intermingle so seamlessly that even Mahound is unable to distinguish between the two. The distinction between the two putatively incompatible identities is hazy enough to enable Rushdie, as Sanga puts it, "to present notions of Self and Other, not as opposite dichotomies but rather as dual entities constantly in dialogue with each other" (39). Or in the terms I have previously suggested, the seemingly opposed tendencies of nationalist identifications and exiled dislocations are, in fact, intertwined with one another. For Rushdie, as Hassumani points out, migrants share the privilege of a "stereoscopic" or inside/outside vision that allows them to maneuver the mainstream from the margins and invent a new way of defining the self, as by "chutnification." As in the Baal episode, social norms are inverted to suggest the falseness created by putting complex concepts such as good and evil into neat frames. Rushdie creates the biography of the imaginary writer, Baal and the role of his "art of metrical slander" that concerns itself with the re-creation or re-presentation of the narrative of Mahound's Islam.

The writer Baal in the Jahilia episode of *The Satanic Verses* is hired by the state of Jahilia to exercise the "art of metrical slander." Pointing to Mahound and his followers, the ruler or Grandee of pre-Islamic Jahilia, Abu Simbel, tells Baal, "That bunch of riff-raff. . . . Those are your targets. Write about them; and their leader, too" (103). In the seventh-century Arabia that is delineated in this section of the novel, Baal perceives the employment of his art for political reasons as degradation. Baal's earlier utopian notion of a poet's art, which, according to him, "is to name the unnamable, to point at frauds, to take sides, start arguments, shape the world, and stop it from going to sleep," now seems impossible (97). At that point the response of the Grandee is to tell Baal that his only alternative is to work as a poet for professional assassins. The trauma of being caught in the dilemma of choosing between the politicization of his art and its vicious commercialization enables Baal to detect the vanity in the desire to pursue "uncontaminated art." Nonetheless, he unsuccessfully tries to resist reducing his art to propaganda. Rushdie goes on to underline the similarity between writers who pursue art for commercial or political reasons and prostitutes who fake love for the purpose of wooing Mammon.

When Mahound returns to Jahilia in his splendor and power after an exile of a quarter-century, Baal is afraid that he will seek vengeance for the wrongs done to him and his followers. Baal is warned that Mahound will not have forgotten Baal's "art of metrical slander," which he had deployed to parody Mahound and his disciples, because "his memory is as long as his face" (375). At this point Baal realizes that the politicization of his art has enervated him: "Baal surveyed his own uselessness, his failed art. Now that he had abdicated all public platforms, his verses were full of loss: of youth, beauty, love, health, innocence, purpose, energy, certainty, hope" (382). As a last resort, however, Baal seeks to hide from Mahound's wrath in the most popular bordello in Jahilia, the Curtain. The Curtain is ruled by the "nameless Madam of the Curtain" whose "guttural utterances from the secrecy of a chair shrouded in black veils had acquired, over the years, something of the oracular" (389). Here, he cohabits with twelve whores. As Baal reminds himself, "until Mahound arrived with his rule book the women dressed brightly, and all the talk was of fucking and money, money and sex, and not just the talk either" (392). So, as a tribute to that bygone era, he encourages his twelve courtesans to each assume the identity of one of Mahound's wives. In a brothel that thrives because of the services of the prophet's wives, the polarized distinction

between the sacred and the profane, harem and brothel, is effectively eliminated, in accordance with Rushdie's consistent practice of challenging
dichotomies or "Manichean binaries."

When finally discovered in the Curtain by Mahound's soldiers, Baal
shouts out, "Whores and writers, Mahound. We are the people you can't for-
give" (329). After the twelve whores are incarcerated, Baal starts sticking his
verses on the walls of the city jail, and on the third day, he uninhibitedly
sings his verses outside the formidable gates of the jail: "Baal sang his love
poems, and the ache in them silenced the other versifiers, who allowed Baal
to speak for them all" (403). Each of his twelve verses is dedicated to each of
his wives, whose names, as previously mentioned, are the same as those of
the prophet's wives. It is at this point that Baal declares, "I recognize no juris-
diction except that of my Muse; or, to be exact, my dozen Muses" (404).

In Baal's composition of eloquent verses the reader perceives the barriers
disintegrating between the real and the unreal, the profane and the sacred.
These barriers are further eroded in Rushdie's portrayal of Baal as Mahound's
shadow self: "Baal stood face to face with the Prophet, mirror facing image, dark
facing light" (391). At his public trial in Islamic Jahilia for writing and reciting
poetry that the new ruler, Mahound, perceives as akin to prostitution, Baal confesses to his marriage to the twelve wives of the Prophet: "The more honestly
and simply Baal described his marriages to the twelve 'wives of the Prophet,' the
more uncontrollable became the horrified mirth of the audience" (404). Baal's
blatant denigration not just of the revealed religion but of the prophet's house
prompts an outraged Mahound to declare, in an outburst that mirrors Baal's
own words, "Writers and whores. I see no difference here," and Baal is sen-
tenced to be decapitated (404).

Baal's deployment of metrical slander to satirize the religion propagated
by Mahound is a variation of Saladin's role as an actor in radio and television
commercials. Unlike Saladin's commercialized art, Baal's slander of Islam and
its prophet is a politicization of his art. But Saladin's ability to play every part
"under a variety of pseudonyms" that the audience cannot tell apart is similar
to Baal's adeptness in mirroring Mahound by playing husband to the twelve
courtesans who impersonate Mahound's wives. Similarly, just as Baal's verse
dismantles the demarcation between the blasphemous and the hallowed, imagination and reality, Gibreel Farishta's portrayal of the anthropomorphized
Hindu pantheon in Indian movies is an intermingling of reality and fantasy.
This dismantling of rigid lines of distinction between carefully rigidified
concepts acknowledges the ambiguity of the space inhabited by the transnational postcolonial subject. The significance of this acknowledgment is that
ethnocentric assumptions that stereotype the immigrant or the transnational

subject and do not allow for porousness in cultural, social, and political boundaries are rendered dysfunctional.

Before the Baal episode, a similar collapse of traditional edifices is reflected in Mahound's quasi-submission to the reigning order in the seventh-century Arabian city of Jahilia. This episode is one of Gibreel's dream narratives that is unraveled in contemporary London. Pre-Islamic Jahilia is a community where various ethnicities, Jewish, Momophysite, Nabataen, come together to trade fabrics from Egypt and China, gold and silver, weaponry and grain. The order that prevails in the city is a kind of Bacchanalian disorder. In this carnivalesque society, poets enjoy a desirable autonomy: as Baal tells the Grandee, "A poet's work is to name the unnamable, to point at frauds, to take sides, start arguments, shape the world, and stop it from going to sleep" (97). Pre-Islamic Jahilia celebrates excess in the form of gambling, dancing, and drinking.

The residents of Jahilia occupy the intersection of the old caravan routes, embodying a node of carnivalesque hybridity. Within this node of hybridity, Rushdie demonstrates a sense of hope about the migrant situation. Even the ancestors of those who dwell in Jahilia are not portrayed as rootless anomalies. On the contrary, for them "the journeying itself was home" (94). These nomads are depicted by the narrator as feeling gratificated and revitalized by the act of traversing territories. But the present inhabitants of the city have evolved from a state of nomadism to one of arrival. The arrival of the migrant suggests, as the narrator observes, "The migrant can do without the journey altogether; it's no more than a necessary evil; the point is to arrive" (94). Thus, *The Satanic Verses* delineates the migrant experience as regenerative and as capable of accomplishing a sense of arrival. The migrant has to undertake a journey in order to arrive in a space of translation and "pickling." The arrival of immigrants in a space that is distinct from their nation of origin places them on a node of hybridity. It enables the erosion of exclusionary politics and the celebration of a place of synthesis where a political order embraces differences—religious, cultural, ethnic—instead of being terrorized by them. Like Saleem's hope of producing "the chutnification of history" in *Midnight's Children*, the migrant who arrives is able to relinquish the impulse to compartmentalize history into "pure" categories of the past, present, and future.

However, Mahound, who had been exiled from Jahilia because of the monotheistic faith he propagated, returns to it at the age of sixty-five, and he is described as a stickler for the rules that he prescribes for every occasion and for every dimension of human life. He finds himself "sprouting rules, rules, rules, until the faithful could scarcely bear the prospect for any more revelations. . . .

Rules about every damn thing" (363). The rules that Mahound imposes on the faithful create a framework that stifles those who subscribe to them. As Rushdie tells us, the city is petrified and rendered callous, "so that it had lost its old, shifting, provisional quality of a mirage and become a prosaic place, quotidian and poor. Mahound's arm had grown long; his powers had encircled Jahilia, cutting off its life-blood, its pilgrims, and caravans" (359–60). Clearly, such passages are unequivocal attempts to oppose dichotomous and rigid perceptions. However, Mahound's yielding to the Grandee's demand of bestowing angelic status on the three favorite goddesses of Jahilia, Al-Lat, Manat, and Uzza, only if it is reciprocated by the wholesale conversion of that region, is presented as an opportunity for Mahound to be flexible about the religion he is propagating.

After the Grandee offers the prophet an opportunity to maintain the venerated status of the three goddesses in exchange for helping Mahound propagate his new faith, Mahound solicits a revelation from Archangel Gibreel that would validate this decision. Later, when Mahound is rethinking this negotiation with the Grandee, he grapples with Gibreel and ultimately allows the Archangel to vanquish him: "After they had wrestled for hours and even weeks Mahound was pinned down beneath the angel, it's what he wanted, it was his will filling me up and giving me strength to hold him down, because archangels can't lose such fights . . ." (123). Subsequently, Mahound reconsiders his negotiation with the Grandee and draws the inference that the verses that prompted him to negotiate with the Grandee of Jahilia were "Satanic" and needed to be expunged in order to maintain the integrity of his monotheistic message. He makes his way to the venerated symbol of Islam, the Kaaba, where he renounces "the foul verses that reek of brimstone and sulphur, to strike them from the record for ever and ever, so that they will survive in just one or two unreliable collections of old traditions and orthodox interpreters will try and rewrite their story" (123). So Mahound retracts his earlier compromise and ends up underscoring his unrelenting posture, which has a profound influence on the kaleidoscopic city of Jahilia. Consequently, Mahound's followers passionately cleave to their iconoclastic beliefs with a passion and raze the Al-Lat temple at Taif.

However, the prophet is chastised for his attitude by the goddess Al-Lat, who causes the illness that leads to his ultimate death. While on his death-bed, Mahound perceives an apparition in his room and he asks, "Is this sickness then thy doing, O Al-Lat?," and the goddess replies, "It is my revenge upon you, and I am satisfied" (406). The ability of Al-Lat to cause the prophet's delirium that precedes his death, together with his acknowledgment of the goddess's presence, suggests that intransigent monotheism offers a fallacious conception of the universe.

The situation is further complicated when Gibreel acknowledges that he did not spout the verses or their condemnation of his own accord, but on the contrary, it was Mahound up to "his old trick, forcing my mouth open and making the voice, the Voice, pour out of me once again" (123). In other words, the doctrine propagated by Mahound is not a divine revelation delivered to him through the interceding authority of the Archangel, but is crafted by the prophet himself. The inauthenticity of the verses is corroborated by Mahound's scribe, Salman the Persian, who states in Gibreel's dream narrative that the religious injunctions were formulated by the mortal Mahound without divine intercession, and only after they were formulated did Gibreel make revelations that entrenched those edicts. The attempt of the institutionalized authority to expunge the satanic verses is indicative of the operating procedure of the fundamentalist discourse of exclusion that relies on tightly drawn boundaries to maintain the "authenticity," or purity, of its discourse.

The power of representation is further undermined in Gibreel's dream about the Imam, which occurs soon after Mahound's migration from Jahilia to the oasis city. Similar to Mahound's, the Imam's version of Islam is uncompromising and intransigent. It rivets around the notion of a monovocal rather than a polyvocal voice. The Imam believes that his version of a pristine Islam is the quintessence of the idea rather than a simulacrum of the notion propounded by Mahound. The Imam, who is an involuntary immigrant from his native land, which he calls "Desh," or homeland, to London, is opposed to images. He is a caricature of Ayatollah Khomeini, who was exiled from Iran to France during the reign of the Shah of Iran. The Imam disavows every simulacra in order to get to the "quintessence" of reality. His refusal to see reality as Rushdie sees it, as a "chutney" with multiple ingredients or as a slippage between various constructions of it seems rather insubstantial considering that even the Imam's ultimate goal, Jerusalem, is a "slippery word . . . It can be an idea as well as a place: a goal, an exaltation. Where is the Imam's Jerusalem?" (212). Rushdie's antithesis to the Imam's radical clericalism is similar to V. S. Naipaul's discomfiture with Ayatollah Khomeini's "new Islamic order" in Iran in the 80s, as articulated in his *Among the Believers.*

The only form of representation that finds favor with the Imam is the postcards bearing "conventional" images of his homeland (206). I would argue that by pointing this out, the author makes clear not just the rigid monotheism of "conventional" Islam but also the inevitable effect of the dominant discourse on the self-construction of subjects. The Imam is portrayed as subscribing to an unyielding set of rules, but he seeks to steer clear of the power that representation can assert. He constrains reality by denying images that do not serve his set of beliefs. There is a satirical reference here to the Islamic prohibition of images of the prophet, his followers, and of God in art.

Furthermore, Rushdie points out that the Imam wants to erase history: "For there is an enemy beyond Ayesha, and it is History herself. History is the blood-wine that must no longer be drunk. History the intoxicant, the creation and possession of the Devil. . . . The greatest of lies—progress, science, rights—against which the Imam has set his face. History is a deviation from the Past, knowledge is a delusion, because the sum of knowledge was complete on the day Al-Lah finished his revelation to Mahound" (210). The multiple narratives inherent in history are anathema to the Imam, whose solace is his refusal to see that the doctrine propounded by Mahound is a construct or an attempt at "chutnified" myth-making just as much as other narratives are. According to the Imam, there can be no slippage between, addition to, or supplement for the knowledge that Al-Lah endowed Mahound with on the day he completed his divine revelation. Once Rushdie divulges that the revelations are myths propagated by Mahound, the idea of knowledge without supplements or slippages is rendered ludicrous. For Rushdie, however, the notion of slippage creates a site of ambivalence on which the hierarchical purity of cultures and other carefully chiseled categories is annulled. The consequent leveling of oppositional categories generates interstices that constitute the terrain for the displacement of clearly defined boundaries.

In order to highlight the profoundly hybrid quality of Rushdie's text, I would deploy Abdul R. JanMohamad's recognition of the richness of literary and cultural "chutnification" that produces a new and distinctive whole. Jan-Mohamad perceives rigid dichotomous categories, specifically those of the colonizer and the colonized, as a Manichean allegory (22). The Manichean allegory in "imaginary texts" is a fetishizing strategy that essentializes the conquered world. Such literature,

> instead of being an exploration of the racial Other affirms its own ethno-centric assumptions; instead of actually depicting the outer limits of "civilization," it simply codifies and preserves the structures of its own mentality. While the surface of each colonialist text purports to represent specific encounters with specific varieties of the racial Other, the subtext valorizes the superiority of European cultures, of the collective process that has mediated that representation. Such literature is essentially specular: instead of seeing the native as a bridge toward syncretic possibility, it uses him as a mirror that reflects the colonialist's self image. (JanMohamad 19)

A writer of the "imaginary" text reinforces an inflexible opposition between the self and the native by retreating to "the homogeneity of his own group" (JanMohamad 20). In other words, despite the recognition of social, political, and cultural differences, the status quo remains unharmed, as in Joyce Cary's *Aissa Saved*. As JanMohamad points out, the narrator of *Aissa Saved* portrays African children who have converted to Christianity as mischievous and irresponsible adults: "Given the colonialist mentality, the source of the contradiction is quite obvious" (21). Such texts do not "contain any syncretic cultural possibility, which alone would open up the historic once more" (JanMohamad 22). The representatives of the discourse of power labor under the illusion that the "civilizing" mission undertaken by them determines the periphery, negating the influence of the periphery on the center. This domain of universal and metaphysical "truths" dehistoricizes dominated peoples and maintains the illusion of a world that has no potential for transnationalism.

On the other hand, writers of "symbolic" texts tend to be more responsive to the notion of the syncretistic "chutnification" of two distinct traditions by creating a modifying dialectic of self and native. As Bill Ashcroft et al. tell us, "according to JanMohamad, it is the ability to bracket the values and bases of imperialist culture that determines the success of the symbolic text and its ability to subvert or avoid the Manichean allegory" (135). JanMohamad subdivides "symbolic" texts into two categories: the first one is represented by novels like E. M. Forster's *A Passage to India* and Rudyard Kipling's *Kim*. These novels attempt to create syncretic solutions to the binary of the colonizer and the colonized, but in certain ways they overlap with the "imaginary" text. Ironically, these novels turn out to be better illustrations of the potency of the Manichean allegory than do the strictly "imaginary" texts.

The second type of "symbolic" fiction is represented by Joseph Conrad's *Heart of Darkness*, because as JanMohamad observes, this work manages to liberate itself from the Manichean allegory by realizing that "syncretism is impossible within the power relations of colonial society because such a context traps the writer in the libidinal economy of the 'imaginary'" (20). So this novel critically examines the "imaginary" mechanism of the colonialist mind-set. In contrast, JanMohamad recognizes literary and cultural syncretism as the domain of third-world writers, stressing the mutuality of cultures. But in order to appreciate colonialist fiction and ideology, JanMohamad propounds the juxtaposition of such fiction with Anglophone fiction of the third-world. This juxtaposition will enable the reader to mark the attempt of third-world literature to engage in a "literary dialogue with

Western cultures" by attempting to "negate the prior European negation of colonized cultures and its adoption and creative modification of Western languages and artistic forms in conjunction with indigenous languages and forms" (23). Rushdie's *Satanic Verses* is an example of this kind of syncretistic fiction that challenges the hierarchy that exists in the host nation and seeks to engage in a dialogic relation with colonialist cultural and social practices.

The consequent tentativeness of oppositional categories in the transnational realm is vividly drawn out for the reader in the "Ayesha" episode of the novel. This episode is one of the magic narratives dreamt by Gibreel. Rushdie explains that this episode is based on an event that occurred in Pakistan in which thirty-eight Shia Muslims walked into the Arabian Sea of their own volition ("In Good Faith" 54). They performed this act of seeming ludicrousness because they expected the waters to part to enable them to make their pilgrimage to Basra in Iraq and from there to the hallowed land of Karbala. This episode is meant to illustrate that Ayesha's religion is conscripted by tightly drawn boundaries and clearly defined laws.

Interestingly enough, Gibreel the Archangel communicates with Ayesha through the medium of popular movie songs, which she interprets as the gospel truth motivating her to lead the pilgrimage across the Indian Ocean to the rallying point of the Islamic faith, Mecca. Her interpretation of the popular film songs sung by Gibreel to gratify her desires is similar to Mahound's interpretation of the words of the Archangel to substantiate his proclamations. Ayesha's unambiguous faith motivates her to lead the congregation that ends up drowning in the Arabian Sea. Her zeal is unmitigated by the protest that "this is the modern world" (232). This protest is made by Mirza Saeed, the husband of one of the converts who proceeds to go on this pilgrimage. Ayesha attempts to solidify Mahound's construction of Islam by believing his concept to be an uncompromising reality.

The illustration of the authority exerted by the discourses of power to construct intransigent categories in the "Ayesha" episode is further foregrounded in the section of the novel entitled "Ellowen Deeowen." After the vertiginous melding of their identities during the fall from the exploded plane, Gibreel and Saladin hurtle into London. In this section, Saladin finds himself transformed into a demonic creature in a grotesque sanitarium. Saladin's metamorphosis changes him from an ordinary mortal into a satyr-like creature with hirsute thighs and legs that taper into cloven hooves. Subsequent to his metamorphosis into a satanic reincarnation, Saladin's alienation is further exacerbated when he is arrested by the British police, who seem to perceive his demonic visage as a social crisis that could disrupt codified structures, if not nipped in the bud. Rushdie points out the social and political significance of the policemen to Saladin's appearance:

> The British authorities, being no longer capable of exporting govern-
> ments, have chosen instead to import a new empire, a new community
> of subject peoples of whom they can think, and with whom they can
> deal, in very much the same way as their predecessors thought of and
> dealt with the fluttered folk and wild, the new-caught sullen peoples,
> half-devil and halfchild. (*Imaginary Homelands* 112)

In this instance, the author opposes the institutionalized authority of the West that represents the transnational subject as a monstrous figure who disrupts the peaceful and constricted existence of the bourgeoisie in London. This authority is similar to the carefully guarded system propagated by Mahound and his devotees. The power of the policemen to label Saladin a freak whose potentially dangerous tendencies can only be curbed by immediate incarceration is put into words by one of the grotesque creatures in the sanitarium while he is there. Saladin finds himself surrounded in his hospital ward by hybrid beings, partly human and partly animal: "men and women who were also partially plants, or giant insects, or even, on occasion, built partly of brick or stone; there were men with rhinoceros horns instead of noses and women with necks as long as any giraffe" (168). This vivid description of the inmates of the hospital ward creates a picture of a menagerie for the reader. His magic realist metamorphosis is interpreted for Saladin by the manticore, a mythical monster with the body and legs of a lion, the face of a man, and a tail, as the power of language to construct conventional images: "They have the power of description, and we succumb to the pictures they construct" (174).

In this section of the book, the conventional portrayal of the immigrant underscores the characterization of the "other" as "primitive" and in need of "civilizing." John Erickson sums up the nature of this constructed "reality" by characterizing the power of description that the manticore refers to as "grounded in a narrative that defines, outlines, and fixes the non-Westerner, turns him into a demonic entity, grotesque and threatening, in need of incarceration in ghettos, detention centers, asylums, and jails" (137). The immigrant, by his or her status as an outsider, serves to reaffirm the system that requires opposition in order to assert itself. Thus, the British officers who arrest Saladin confer "with solemn faces and judicious voices," of the need, "in this day and age, for an increase in observation, not merely in the sense of 'spectating,' but in that of 'watchfulness,' and 'surveillance'".

The manticore goes on to tell Saladin that there was a woman in the ward who was now "mostly water-buffalo," a group of Nigerian businessmen who had grown "sturdy tails," and a group of holiday-makers from Senegal who were transformed into slippery snakes while changing planes. Prior to his transformation, the manticore himself was a highly sought-after male model in Bombay. In a passage that recalls René Descartes' *Meditations* and prefigures Saladin's dreams, the manticore also points out a woman to Saladin whose skin was turned to glass, commenting that "the bastards smashed it up for her" (Rushdie 174).

The generation of Manichean oppositions in the sanitarium instigates the immigrant consciousness to rebel against representation. Because of the hopelessness in the Detention Centre, the manticore and some of the other creatures decide to flee the premises: "The monsters ran quickly, silently, to the edge of the Detention Centre compound, where the manticore and other sharp-toothed mutants were waiting by the large holes they had bitten into the fabric of the containing fence, and then they were out, free, going their separate ways, without hope, but also without shame" (176). The ostracized denizens of the hospital ward represent the excluded and repressed immigrant consciousness.

The fragmentation of the displaced subject reduces him or her to a rubble involving the "debris of the soul, broken memories, sloughed-off selves, severed mother-tongues, violated privacies, untranslatable jokes and extinguished fires" (4). In this world, "What follows is tragedy," or at least a "burlesque for our degraded, imitative times" (397). For instance, in the last of the London sections, "The Angel Azraeel," an inversion is caused in the Asian ghetto in London. This is a world that Saladin is unfamiliar with because it does not coincide with his glamorous world of the polished Oxbridge accent and the country club of polite superficialities. On the contrary, the ghetto is inhabited by individuals who do not fit the mold of what he recognized as civilized and rational English. In this seamy subterranean region, unspeakable atrocities are inflicted on individuals because of the color of their skin and blatant racism leads to false charges of murder against a radical leader of the Asian community. In this sordid atmosphere, an allegation of assault is leveled against a fifty-year-old Nigerian woman while she is beaten black and blue. The vociferous protests of local black youths to the unsubstantiated allegation leveled at the vulnerable immigrant are not looked upon favorably by the authorities. The representatives of the law-enforcing machinery, the British police, undertake to harass these protesting youths by routinely abducting, bludgeoning and mauling them, and finally flinging these maimed individuals back into the streets.

Implicit in this dissention of the Asian community is loyalty to an immigrant who is allegedly a demented serial killer. However, this form of egregious protest is also an allegiance to race polarization, which Rushdie attempts to undercut despite his sympathies with the motivation behind it. This sort of unmitigated hate is hostile to the generation of diverse possibilities of interpretation that are perpetuated by the immigrants' "perspective of their cultural heterogeneity and hybridity" (Boehmer 173).

The London that Saladin is exposed to in the Asian ghetto harbors an unglamorous and marginalized subculture that he had tried his utmost to shun. This hostile and unwelcoming city is explicitly described by the owner of an illegal bed-and-breakfast establishment in the ghetto, Hind, as "a demon city in which anything could happen":

> your windows shattered in the middle of the night without any cause, you were knocked over in the middle of the street by invisible hands, in the shops you heard such abuse you felt your ears would drop off, when you turned in the direction of the words you saw only empty air and smiling faces, and every day you heard about this boy, that girl, beaten up by ghosts. Yes, a land of phantom imps, how to explain. (Rushdie 250)

The racial harassment inflicted on London's immigrant community is a phantasmagoric attempt to preserve the "unsullied" façade of the institutions of the former imperial power by endangering the existence of any people who differ from the English. Despite his identification with that power, the grime and filth of the ghetto make cracks in Saladin's veneer of Englishness, and he feels his adopted identity slipping through his fingers like fine grains of sand.

The demonization of Saladin, which leads to his incarceration in the Detention Centre and eventually causes him to sever his ties with his country of adoption, erodes his former resolution to disavow the culture into which he was born. Zeeny's veneration of bricolage is unambiguous and ends up influencing Saladin. As a bricoleur, Zeeny works with concepts and ideas retrieved from the past in order to create "chutnified" or improvisatory products. She collects bits and pieces of the intellectual materials that different eras supply:

> Zeeny is an art critic whose book on the confining myth of authenticity, that folkloristic straitjacket which she sought to replace by an ethic of historically validated eclecticism, for was not the entire national culture based on the principle of borrowing whatever clothes seemed to fit, Aryan, Mughal, British, take-the-best-and-leave-the-rest. (52)

Saladin imbibes this ethic and comes to terms with his past by reconciling with his father, who embodies Saladin's childhood in India. Unlike Gibreel, he manages to survive because he is able to form an identity that encompasses his past and his present.

Similarly, in his next novel, *Haroun and the Sea of Stories* (1990), by allowing his protagonist, Haroun, to recognize the unwholesomeness of dualities, Rushdie propagates the syncretism of two distinct conventions, Speech and Silence, in order to conceive a new whole.

Rushdie continues to amalgamate myth with history in order to undermine institutionalized beliefs in his next novel, *The Moor's Last Sigh* (1995). As Rushdie observes in *Imaginary Homelands,* "History is always ambiguous. Facts are hard to establish, and capable of being given many meanings" (25). *The Moor's Last Sigh* evoked an ire similar to the one provoked by the publication of *The Satanic Verses.* It was not released for distribution in Bombay by its Indian publisher for fear of inciting violence. In this novel, the author caricatures Bal Thackeray, the nationalist leader of one of the cohorts of the second largest political party in India, the Bharatiya Janata Party, which has Hindu fundamentalist leanings. Bombay is a stronghold of this party. Subsequently, the novel was banned in India for a short while, but the ban was officially removed a couple of months later.

In this novel as in his other works, Rushdie questions the resurgence of fundamentalist interests and the social, cultural, and political struggles related to it. It is the lack of this "chutnification" of history in *Shame* that causes the nation-state of Pakistan to be "insufficiently imagined" (20). In his novel about the post-independence Indian subcontinent, *Shame,* Rushdie elucidates the situation of the migrant in its glory as well as in its hopelessness:

> When individuals come unstuck from their native land, they are called migrants. What is the best thing about migrant peoples? I think it is their hopefulness. Look into the eyes of such folk in old photographs. Hope blazes undimmed through the fading sepia tints. And what's the worst thing? It is the emptiness of one's luggage. I'm speaking of invisible suitcases, not the physical, perhaps cardboard variety containing a few meaning-drained mementos: we have come unstuck from more than land. We have floated upwards from history, from memory, from Time. (91)

The politics of cultural survival is hostile to a liberalism of rights that insists on the uniform application of rights and collective goals. Such uniformity is oblivious to the aspirations of distinct societies and to the variations in laws from one cultural context to another: "Liberalism is not a possible meeting ground for all cultures, but is the political range of one range of cultures, and quite incompatible with other ranges" (Taylor 95). At times, Rushdie's celebratory discourse of hybridity comes dangerously close to a liberalism that claims to be a neutral ground on which peoples of different cultures can coexist, but which is in fact a reflection of one hegemonic culture.

Despite the glories of migration, imperial ideology marks immigrants as inferior. As a strategy to debunk their marginal status, immigrants then generate a "position for reconstruction" (Boehmer 117). Saladin Chamcha is an embodiment of the reconstructed position of the immigrant. For the immigrant, there remain "old selves, old selves erased in part but not fully. So what you get are these fragmented, multifaceted, multicultural selves" (Marzorati 44). Significantly, *The Satanic Verses* is the embodiment of a world in which boundaries have been blurred to create a palimpsest from which one facet of the self has been partially erased in order to make room for the other, and the reader, as Rushdie articulates, is cast into "the world beyond the looking glass, where nonsense is the only sense" ("Pen Against the Sword" 57). Thus, Rushdie consciously explores a radical sense of otherness, which is heightened for immigrants as a consequence of displacement.

As opposed to the irresolvability of polarities in *Shame*, *The Satanic Verses* embodies the mix of contemporary-historical and mythical-religious contexts. The various layers that compose identity, the simultaneous production of good and evil, different historical periods, different locations, different personalities, and various states of consciousness interact with one another in the novel.

Chapter Four

Citizenship in a Transnational Age: Culture and Politics in Ghosh's *The Shadow Lines*

> I think the difference between the history historians write and the history fiction writers write is that fiction writers write about the human history. It's about finding the human predicament, it's about finding what happens to individuals, characters. I mean that's what fiction is. . . . Exploring both dimensions, whereas history, the kind of history exploring causes, causality, is of no interest to me. (Ghosh, "Shadow Script" 30)

Amitav Ghosh's *The Shadow Lines* is an attempt to give voice to the stony silences and exhume the unclaimed corpses in the catacombs of "unhistorical historiography" (Guha 1). Many aspects of the eras of the Partition of 1947 and the further partition of 1971 are repressed into the political unconscious of the people of the Indian subcontinent. In this novel, Ghosh not only presents the reader with a political vision that questions the ethnolinguistic and cultural divides created by the fiery resurgence of nationalist ideologies, but interweaves that vision with the human story he delineates in the novel. In other words, the author seeks to elaborate on the larger politics of postcolonialism in affirming the identities of common people and their cultural anchors.

Ghosh has published novels that continue to gain critical acclaim in their attempt to establish the processes of citizenship and diasporic identity formation as one of perpetual struggle. His first novel, *The Circle of Reason* (1986), won the Prix Medici Estranger, one of France's most prestigious awards. Ghosh's second novel, *The Shadow Lines* (1988), won the Sahitya Akademi award, India's most renowned literary prize. According to Edward

Hower of the *New York Times Book Review,* Ghosh's second novel is "a stunning book—amusing, sad, and truly international in scope" (10). And Mary Cuoto endorses that verdict by declaring that, "in *The Shadow Lines,* Ghosh has found his own distinctive voice—polished and profound" (1212). Since then, he has published *In an Antique Land* (1993), *The Calcutta Chromosome* (1995), and *The Glass Palace* (2001). The ability of Ghosh's texts to draw on various cultural traditions, along with his own diasporic subjectivity as an Indian of Burmese origin who was raised in Bangladesh, Iran, Sri Lanka, has done his writing in Egypt, and now does it in the U.S., corresponds well with the subjects of emigration, exile, and cultural displacement addressed in his work. His diasporic subjectivity and the subject matter of his fiction have led many critics to see him as a blossoming postcolonial writer. Ghosh's work is a crucial component of Western literary studies classified as "Postcolonial Studies."

In *The Shadow Lines,* I argue that Ghosh interrogates the authenticity of colonial and nationalist historiography by, on the one hand, emphasizing the fictions that people create in their lives, and, on the other, recording the vivid and verifiable details of individual memories that do not necessarily correspond with the documented version of history. As the narrator says, "stories are all there are to live in, it was just a question of which one you chose" (15). This finding enables the narrator to come to grips with the "deterritorialization of culture" (Appadurai 10), the way in which the affinity between the members of a community is sustained despite geographical divides that might separate them as citizens of different countries. It is only as an adult historian that the narrator is able to integrate fragments of his memory into a composite whole. He articulates his journey down memory lane for the reader, it is "sitting in the air-conditioned calm of an exclusive library" that he begins his strangest journey: "a voyage into a land outside space, an expanse without distances; a kind of looking glass event" (224).

As works like Amitav Ghosh's *Shadow Lines,* Salman Rushdie's *Satanic Verses,* and Anita Desai's *In Custody* show, the Indian novel in English is an exploration of the historical transformations of community life: "Instead of drawing Jamesian 'portraits' of sensitive individuals, this type of novel attempts to project a vision of the individual under the community, the individual under the sway of larger movements of history" (Mukherjee 24). Interestingly enough, the conventions that Raymond Williams would like to see the English novel subscribe to are manifested in the novels of writers like Rushdie, Naipaul, Desai, and Ghosh: "Not selected persons, not persons composed in a single life's trajectory or around an idea or a theme; but there in the way neighbors are, friends are, the people we work with are" (143). By confronting burning social and political issues of their times created by transnational cultural, political, and economic flows, these transnational writers deploy their sensibilities, one Western and one homegrown, to engage in a dialogical relationship with society and to overcome restraints that deradicalize the literary works of the "Third-World." Ghosh remains engaged with his cultural and historical past throughout the novel by rejecting the process of historicizing the imperial past in favor of personal memory and imagination.

I argue that although *Shadow Lines* does take a rather limited and restrictive view of nationalism by portraying the concept of the nation as an invention that breeds heinous crimes and relentless violence, Ghosh does not portray his characters as existential individuals pursuing spiritual journeys in order to find their individual epiphanies. On the contrary, he treats his characters as individuals molded and confronted by their cultural and sociopolitical environment. Ghosh's characters encounter a new world, a new cultural paradigm while trying to preserve their own recognizable forms of identity. His agenda is to threaten the safely-guarded domain of privilege and power by demanding equality for human beings of all races, religions, cultures, and ethnicities. Ghosh's stance raises some interesting issues: What is his position vis-à-vis the volatile political situation in the Indian subcontinent? Does the novel suggest a viable alternative to the terrors of nationalism? Does it deal with the complexities of universalism?

The author creates a realm that melds pre-Independence India, Britain in the Second World War, and post-Independence India. Deploying this realm as one of intermingling cultural and political paradigms and ideologies as well as of overlapping geographical divides, Ghosh undertakes the task of establishing the futility of all sorts of barriers, or "shadow lines." As one of the Subaltern Studies scholars, Shail Mayaram, reminds us, during the Partition of India various state authorities rigidified borders and boundaries that were once flexible, and people were coerced to opt for one nation or the other, India or Pakistan, or one religious identity or the other, Hindu or Muslim. And in many cases the choice was imposed on them (128). There are other novels in Indo-English fiction that belong to the Partition genre: Khushwant Singh's *A Train to Pakistan* (1956), Manohar Malgonkar's *A Bend in the Ganges* (1965), Raj Gill's *The Rape* (1974), Balachandra Rajan's *The Dark Dancer* (1970), and Bapsi Sidhwa's *Ice-Candy-Man* (1988). *Shadow Lines*, however, is especially notable because it delineates the agonies and ruptures of that period in such poignant detail. It also underlines the challenge of cultural dislocations, ambiguous citizenship, and highlights the illusions of militant nationalisms.

The unnamed narrator's nationalist grandmother, Tha'mma, articulates an unambiguous understanding of the central role of violence in the making of nations in *The Shadow Lines* when she talks about the creation of Britain:

> It took those people a long time to build that country; hundreds of years, years and years of war and bloodshed. They know they're a nation because they've drawn their borders with blood. Hasn't Maya told you how regimental flags hang in all their cathedrals and how all their churches are lined with memorials to men who died in wars, all around the world? War is their religion. That's what it takes to make a country. Once that happens people forget they were born this or that, Muslim or Hindu, Bengali or Punjabi: they become a family born of the same pool of blood. That is what you have to achieve for India, don't you see? (77–8)

And yet, as Ghosh shows, the nation is rendered all the more threatening when the war that leads to its construction is internecine and does not bind Muslim to Hindu or Bengali to Kashmiri but rather sunders Bengali from Bengali, Kashmiri from Kashmiri. Such an irregular war polarizes these ethnic groups into Hindus and Muslims who are required to disaffirm their cultural, linguistic, and social unities. As one of the characters in Ghosh's novel wonders, "And then I think to myself why don't they draw thousands of little lines through the whole subcontinent and give every little place a new name? What would it change? It's a mirage; the whole thing is a mirage. How can anyone divide a memory?" (247).

Ghosh's *Shadow Lines* narrates the story of three generations of the unnamed narrator's family, spread over Dhaka, Calcutta, and London. The narrative begins in colonial India and concludes just after the creation of East Pakistan in the '60s. The story highlights private and public events and their significance as they bring the characters into relief. *The Shadow Lines* describes a period that goes back to colonial India, prior to the birth of the narrator. A cousin of the narrator's father, Tridib, has witnessed the gruesome Partition of India and the corollary creation of Pakistan in 1947.[1] He, therefore, hankers after a place "where there was no border between oneself and one's image in the mirror" (29). The image in the mirror is a poignant reference to that segment of the population that has either fled or been made to flee to the newly created nation-state of Pakistan. The novel begins with a passage about the happenings in colonial India: "In 1939, thirteen years before I was born, my father's aunt, Mayadebi, went to England with her husband and her son, Tridib" (3). The plot begins in the year 1939 during the chaos of the Second World War and ends in 1964 with the political upheaval caused by the outbreak of communal riots in India and Pakistan.

The story revolves around Tridib, who is taken to England by his parents in 1939, at the age of eight, and then in 1964 is a victim of communal frenzy in Dhaka. As the opening sentence indicates, the beginning of the narrative takes place thirteen years before the narrator's birth, and thus his knowledge of the ravages of the Second World War comes to him through Tridib's recapitulations. The details of Tridib's death are given to him years later by Tridib's brother, Roby, and his girlfriend, May Price. Price was a witness to the inexplicable frenzy and violence that resulted in his death. This horrific occurrence is linked with the catastrophic political events in England and on the Indian subcontinent that the narrator attempts to understand cohesively. The narrative is a search "for the elusive formal and causal logic that will allow the narrator's autobiography (and equally the national biography that is interwoven with it in the novel) to cohere, to make sense" (Kaul, "Separation Anxiety" 42). Thus two instances of the devastating force of the fervor of nationalism in 1939 and 1964 mark the narrator's growth from childhood to adulthood.

Through Tridib and his niece, Ila, and their relationship with the Price family, the narrative captures the past by describing a London rent apart by WWII and then bounds back to the present by describing a time when the narrator is himself a student in London. Additionally, through the narrator's grandmother, Tha'mma, with her East Bengali background and memories of her childhood days in Dhaka, the narrative takes the reader back in time to the era prior to the Partition, and through her fateful return to her original home in search of her uncle, Jethamoshai, it makes the reader aware of the calamitous consequences of the Partition. The political and social upheaval that followed upon the creation of the nation-states of India and Pakistan in 1947 has left legacies that continue to haunt the two countries.[2] The Partition enabled the thunderous forces of violence and displacement to tear the preexisting cultural and social fabric so systematically that the process of repair hasn't even begun.

I would argue that although the "Third-World" intelligentsia unceasingly complains about the manipulations and short-sightedness of British imperial cartographers and administrators, the onus of the calamity engendered on 14 and 15 August 1947 does not lie entirely on the colonial power. The failed negotiations between "Indian" and "Pakistani" nationalists who belonged to the Congress and the Muslim League, the blustering of those nationalists and the national jingoism it stimulated, and the unquenchable hatreds on both sides contributed to the brutal events of 1947. In the words of historian Uma Kaura, "the mistakes made by the Congress leadership, the frustration and bitterness of the League leadership, and the defensive diplomacy of a British Viceroy cumulatively resulted in the demand for partition" (170). As Kaura points out, ever since the inception of pro-independence political activity in pre-Partition India in 1885, the Muslim leadership insisted on the necessity for a distinct Muslim identity (164). Kaura also underlines the inability of the nationalist leadership to accommodate Muslim aspirations because its primary concern was to ingratiate itself with the militant Hindu faction, which could have created unmendable dissensions within the Congress (165).

The borders that were brutally carved by the authorities at the time of Partition have led to further brutality in the form of those riots, pogroms, and organized historical distortions and cultural depletions with which the history of independent India is replete. Hindu as well as Muslim leaders, according to Kaul bear responsibility for those events:

> There are stories that have been told so often, including by historians, that they have become the official memory of Partition itself. Each time we teach the story of Partition in order to demonstrate . . . the culpability of the Muslim League, and ignore the role played by religious chauvinists within the Congress or other political and social organizations, we tell a tale that deepens the divides signified by Partition. (*Partitions* 5)

It is an unfortunate fact that all the historical and social events that led to the catastrophe of 1947 can best be understood within the explanatory frameworks of religious and familial obligation. This molding of collective subjectivities by the evocation of pan-national religious affinities results in the stifling of minority voices that express divergent cultural and social opinions. The narrator of Ghosh's *Shadow Lines* observes, "As always, there were innumerable cases of Muslims in East Pakistan giving shelter to Hindus, often at the cost of their own lives, and equally in India of Hindus sheltering Muslims" (229–30). Such people demonstrate the "indivisible sanctity that binds people to each other independently . . . , for it is in the logic of states that to exist at all they must claim the monopoly of all relationships between peoples" (230). Since these two nations were founded on the ineradicable idea of religious difference, the religious agendas of fundamentalist groups now rule over the Indian subcontinent.

In addition, "official" accounts of the Partition discount narratives that do not contribute to the deepening of the breach caused by the fracture lines of nationalist collective subjectivity and religious identity.[3] This exclusionary tactic deployed by nationalist historiography, according to which the populace of the Indian subcontinent was a passive recipient of the repercussions of the nationalist struggle valiantly fought by the Western-educated elite, is articulately interrogated in the inaugural statement in *Subaltern Studies I*: "What is clearly left out of the un-historical historiography is the politics of the people" (Guha 1).

I observe that the Partition is a vivid manifestation of the claim that postcolonial nations are founded in a bloody severance of the umbilical cord, one that fortifies borders between nation-states with irrational and remorseless violence. The discourse of nationalism, however, affects to make sense of the absurd loss of lives that occurs. As the narrator of *The Shadow Lines* ruminates on the etching of boundaries and partitions,

> They had drawn their borders, believing in that pattern, in the enhancement of lines, hoping perhaps that once they had etched their borders upon the map, the two bits of land would sail away from each other like the shifting tectonic plates of the prehistoric Gondwanaland. What had they felt, I wondered, when they discovered that they had created not separation, but a yet un-discovered irony. (232)

In his novel Ghosh negotiates the space of cultural difference by drawing analogies and suggesting similarities among emotions, sensibilities, and abodes. For instance, Mrs. Price's house in London, with its fascinating cellar, is almost identical to Tridib's ancestral Raibajar house, with its "cavernous" underground room. For Tridib's niece, Ila, this room with its "looming shrouded shapes" evokes memories of the cellar in Mrs. Price's house, in which she played with her son, Nick. It is interesting that when the adult narrator finally visits the Price house, which he had so often constructed in his mind's eye, he realizes that he would never be able to reconstruct the picture that Tridib had painted for him: "Just as one may watch a tree for months and yet know nothing at all about it if one happens to miss that one week when it bursts into bloom" (57).

He goes to London on a one-year research grant in order to collect archival material from the India Office Library to work on a dissertation on the nineteenth-century textile trade between India and England. While in that house, the narrator finds himself alone with Ila on two occasions in the underground room, and each time, it reminds him of the opulent house in Calcutta with its cavernous room. He recalls that while in that room, he had constructed Nick Price as his mirror image but one that he longed to eclipse because that image was enviable in its presumed English gracefulness. Although the narrator as a child hadn't seen Nick, he tells us that Nick "became a spectral presence beside [him] in the looking-glass, growing with [him] but always bigger and better, and in some ways more desirable" (50).

The narrator confesses that the apparition had been an overwhelming presence and had haunted him throughout his adolescence: "I would look into the glass and there he would be growing, always faster, always a head taller than me" (50). In addition to representing a lingering sense of Indian subjection to England, the unwavering obsession with Nick is a reflection of the narrator's feelings for Ila. As he tells us, "I looked at Ila, at her finely-planed, high-cheekboned face, her long, brown eyes, and her shining-black hair, curling down to her shoulders, and she felt my gaze on her. . . . And so, as always, it was Ila—Ila of whom it was said when we were children, that she and I were so alike that I could have been her twin" (31).

The narrator's obsession with Nick is also indicative of the fictiveness of the national boundaries that get blurred in imaginations like his and Tridib's. Tridib explains to the narrator, "[O]ne could never know anything except through desire, real desire, which was not the same thing as greed or lust; a pure, painful and primitive desire, a longing for everything that was not in oneself, a torment of the flesh that carried one beyond the limits of one's mind to other times and other places" (29). I see Tridib as being painfully aware of the unfathomable depth of the human mind that requires the individual to pursue an infinite and interminable search for the knowledge that would disrupt all-encompassing religious narratives and demystify the production of conceptions nurtured by sectarianism and nationalism.

At the same time, Tridib cannot elude his cognizance of "the seductive clarity of ignorance; an illusion of knowledge created by the deceptive weight of remembered detail" (67). While in London, he contemplates the anticipated repercussions of WWII and the destinies of Mrs. Price's brother, Alan, and his three friends. Tridib realizes that this blissful ignorance enables one to evade the starkest of realities, the reality of death that he perceives not only in London but also during the 1964 Hindu-Muslim riots in India and Pakistan:

> The realities of the bombs and torpedoes and the dying was easy enough to imagine—mere events, after all, recorded in thousands of films and photographs and comic books. But not that infinitely more important reality: the fact that they knew, that even walking down that street, that evening, they knew what was coming—not the details nor the timing perhaps, but they knew, that their world, and in all probability they themselves, would not survive the war. . . . Nobody knows, nobody can ever know, not even in memory, because there are moments in time that are not knowable: nobody can ever know what it was like to be young and intelligent in the summer of 1939 in London or Berlin. (67–8)

Tridib's story is a defiance of meta-narratives, because human knowledge will always be tentative and arbitrary. He inspires the narrator to construct his own narratives in order to avoid getting incarcerated in someone else's oppressive stories that reflect ethnic and religious jealousies and rivalries. He is warned that the alternative to inventing one's own story "wasn't blankness—it only meant that if we didn't try ourselves, we should never be free of other people's inventions" (31).

Tridib adds to the child narrator's repertoire by regaling him with fascinating discourses on Eastern European jazz, the habits of arboreal apes, the plays of Garcia Lorca, and the archaeological sites associated with the Sena dynasty of Bengal. He augments and embellishes the child narrator's sensibility by telling him that around the Raibajar house near Calcutta, rainforests had been imported from Brazil and the Congo: "The house had vanished behind a forest that stretched all the way up the knoll, the trees growing so thick and close together that they hid the house like a curtain. Tridib, grinning, told [him] to take a good look, for [he] wouldn't see trees like those again for a long time: his grandfather had wanted to live in a tropical rainforest so he'd imported those trees from Brazil and the Congo" (45). This exposure to the geographical inclusiveness constructed by the transnational global economy locates the narrator specifically in his cultural milieu but also renders the nation a mutable concept. The mutability of the nation is a novel concept for the narrator as a child who, as he says, believed "in the reality of space." He goes on to say, "I believed that distance separates, that it is a corporeal substance; I believed in the realities of nations and borders; I believed that across the border there existed another reality" (219). But his perception is metamorphosed by the events in the novel.

As the critic A. N. Kaul points out, the predominant theme of *The Shadow Lines* is the crossing of frontiers of nationality, culture, and language in three countries: India, East Pakistan (now Bangladesh), and England (303). To that list, I would add the author's attempt to cross the barrier of citizenship as a self-conscious political philosophy. Ghosh makes the reader aware of the humanist response to the ridiculousness of war, a response that transcends national boundaries and barriers.[4] Tridib's desire to dismantle boundaries created by nation-states is unequivocal in the letter he writes to May Price, expressing his desire to meet her "in a place without a past, without history, free, really free, two people coming together with the utter freedom of strangers" (232). It is through Tridib's artfully woven yarns that the narrator learns to traverse spaces created by political, cultural, and socioeconomic differences. He tells the narrator enthralling tales of imaginative and real journeys while pointing out the countries in the time-worn

Bartholomew Atlas: "Tridib had given me whole worlds to travel in and he had given me eyes to see them with" (20). The visions fashioned for him by Tridib, long before the narrator actually moves out of Calcutta, enable his world to grow beyond the confines of his native land to include unseen points on the Atlas: Cairo, Madrid, Cuzco or Colombo. The narrator's intellectual horizon is further widened by the exotic tales brought back by Tridib's niece, Ila, from far-off domains like Bratislava, Konarky, and Sophia, as well as by the autobiographical details of May Prices's maternal grandparents, the Tresawsens' travels in locales like Malaysia, Fiji, Bolivia, the Guinea Coast, and Ceylon, related by May Price, the granddaughter of Lionel Tresawsen, who had lived in India in the epoch of the British Raj and had been a friend of Tridib's grandfather.

But unlike Tridib, Ila is unable to reject official versions of history. She does not share the narrator's fascination for the locales to which she has traveled. As Murari Prasad points out, "Her dislocation stems from her penchant for illusions devoid of any real understanding of the cultural interface" (93). I would observe that Ila is unable to take the knowledges from the dispossessed peoples of the world as seriously as she does those of the West. Ila reduces the mesmerizing quality of Cairo to a place where the ladies restroom was on the other side of the departure lounge. As the narrator beratingly tells her, "To you Cairo was a place to piss in" (21). The narrator observes that for Ila "the current was the real: it was as though she lived in a present which was like an airlock in a canal, shut away from the tidewaters of the past and the future by steel floodgates" (30). Her experience of different countries and cultures is interred in the yearbooks of the international schools that she attended as a child: "Those schools were all that mattered to Ila; the places themselves went past her in an illusory whirl of movement" (23). Ila cannot move beyond the confines of the knowledge that is sanctioned within unsullied academic premises. And places and experiences that enthralled the narrator were uninteresting as far as Ila was concerned. The narrator makes that clear when he points out that in listening to her talking to her father and grandfather "about the cafés in the Plaza Mayor in Madrid, or the crispness of the air in Cuzco, [he] could see that those names, which were to [him] a set of magical talismans because Tridib had pointed them out to [him] on his tattered old Bartholomew's Atlas, had for her a familiarity no less dull than the Lake had for [him] and [his] friends; the same tired intimacy that made us stop on our way back from the park in the evening and unbutton our shorts and aim our piss through the rusty wrought-iron railings" (20). When the narrator goes to London a decade later, he observes that her loyalty to the present has been augmented in her adulthood.

As an adult in England, nothing can shake Ila's confidence that history can only happen in Europe because whatever catastrophic events occur in India, Malaysia, or Nigeria "are only local things after all—not like revolutions or anti-fascist wars, nothing that sets a political example to the world, nothing that's really remembered" (105). Her internalized self-loathing and precarious transplantation into British culture make her scream out at her uncle in rage that she wants to renounce the fetters of Indian culture: "Free of your bloody culture and free of all of you" (89).

According to her, life in an obscure Third-World country deprived one of the joy of being part and parcel of global movements. She is unaware of the ruthless reality of the postcolonial who, in certain instances, is forcibly dismembered from her/his land and made to encounter a world that is disfigured by war and famine. She is careful to remind the narrator that he has led a cloistered and bland existence in the suburbs of Delhi and Calcutta, so he "can't know what this kind of happiness means: there's a joy merely in knowing that you're a part of history" (104). Ila deludes herself into believing that residence in the "mother country," England, entitled one to feel "a part of the important events of their time—the war, and fascism, all the things you read about today in history books." Ila's self-loathing prods her to tell the narrator in no uncertain terms that "nothing really important happens where you are" (104).

Even the cold shoulder that Ila gets from her activist acquaintances, who treat her as a superficial, well-manicured addition to their anti-Nazi league, does nothing to dispel her deluded state of mind. The narrator gives us a glimpse into the character of the activist politics that Ila is involved in: "I had been with Ila once, when she had come out of her hairdresser's shop, her hair all new and curled, and marched straight off to Brixton with her little crew of friends, to confront a gang of jack-booted racists armed with bicycle chains" (105). The narrator compares this picture of a well-groomed Ila strutting to Brixton to the lives of young people in Calcutta, who had been raised in the engulfing religious and sectarian violence of the sixties and seventies, and Ila's courage pales by comparison. Ila's lop-sided political activism negates the interests of native Indian peoples. Meenakshi Mukherjee sums up the character as one who "has always wanted to belong either as blue-eyed Magda or as a trendy Marxist" (263). The blue-eyed and flaxen-haired Magda doll in the Tresawsens' cellar represents the earlier Ila, who prefers the English Nick Price to the Indian narrator. She fantasized that Nick was in love with the Magda doll.[5]

Thus, Ila rationalizes the isolation that she is subjected to in European schools by conjuring an image of herself as an immensely popular member of the group of the most desirable young women. As the narrator says, "Ila's closest friends were the most beautiful, the most talented, the most intelligent girls in the school. She would point them out to me in the pictures of picnics and fancy-dress dances." But he can't help noticing that "though Ila could tell [him] every-thing about those parties and dances, what she did and what she wore, she herself was always unaccountably absent in the pictures" (22). The illusions that Ila fosters in order to conceal her vulnerability are a consequence of her negative self-image, which has a psychological force that determines her behavior as a response to European domination. In order to break free of any ties that might bind her further to India, Ila seeks validation from the "mother country" by marrying Nick Price. She is soon wracked by Nick's infidelities and is disillusioned by the realization that "the squalor of the genteel little lives she had so much despised was a part of the free world she had tried to build for herself" (188).

The novel not only underlines the challenge of cultural dislocations but also highlights the illusions of militant nationalisms. For instance, although the nationalism of the narrator's grandmother, Tha'mma, is portrayed as a contrast to Ila's anglophilia, it is nevertheless an equally inadequate master myth that leaves those who subscribe to it in a vulnerable state. So we learn when, while reminiscing about her childhood, Tha'mma relates the story of a timid bearded boy who had been in college with her in Dhaka, the capital of post-1971 Bangladesh, in the era prior to the Partition. She describes him as a reserved and bashful person who lived in their neighboring lane in Dhaka's Potua-tuli. He was a self-conscious and reticent student with a low profile. Tha'mma recalls that one morning during a class, a posse of policemen stormed into the classroom and subdued the protesting lecturer as well as the students. The English officer looked around the room carefully, scanning the faces of the students and comparing them with the picture that he had in his hand. After what seemed like an eternity, the officer focused his gaze on the self-effacing boy in the back of the classroom, and he was hand-cuffed and escorted out of the room in the presence of his disbelieving classmates. It is later discovered that the boy had been a member of a clandestine terrorist network since the age of fourteen. He was well trained in the use of weaponry and ammunition. As Tridib explains to the unknowing child narrator, in the early nineteenth century there was a terrorist movement among nationalists in Bengal. The covert terrorist societies like Anushilan and Jugantar planned operations to subvert the rule of the British in colonial India. But Tha'mma's classmate's training and his mission to assassinate an English magistrate proved useless after his arrest, because "that boy was tried and later deported to the infamous Cellular Gaol in the Andaman Islands" (38). Tha'mma confesses that knowledge of the boy's clandestine activities had fascinated her and caused her to glorify him:

> Ever since she heard those stories, she had wanted to do something for the terrorists, work for them in a small way, steal a little bit of their glory for herself. She would have been content to run their errands for them, to cook their food, wash their clothes, anything. . . . if only she had known, if only she had been working with him, she would have warned him somehow, she would have saved him. . . . (39)

Tha'mma's flame of nationalist fervor blazes with so much passion that she declares without flinching that if she had known about her timid classmate's furtive mission, she would have helped him to kill the English magistrate as a momentous step toward freedom: "yes, I would have killed him. It was for our freedom: I would have done anything to be free" (39).

Her concept of nationalism deploys the idea of citizenship and fraternity that unifies the entire community in the pursuit of a common goal. Her notion can be elucidated by Eric Hobsbawm's analysis of the unprecedented rise of new nationalisms. As Hobsbawm argues, nationalism establishes an inclusion/exclusion dichotomy in which those who belong can be winnowed away from those who are outsiders. He observes that this binary was reinforced by the nation-state most forcefully in the post-Cold War era of post-colonialism, post-communism, and post-history. He points out that in the age of transnationalism, the social coherence created by the nation totters and, in certain cases, gets demolished. However, Hobsbawm argues, the breach caused by the depletion of the nation is filled by ethnicity, which forms the individual's new epistemic perspective. Within a similar framework of inclusion/exclusion, Tha'mma argues that Ila will always be a misfit in England because "everyone who lives there has earned his right to be there with blood: with their brother's blood and with their father's blood and their son's blood. They know they are a nation because they have drawn their borders with blood" (78). In order to assert itself a nation-state needs to draw clearly etched borders so it can define itself in opposition to other nations. But I would point out that Tha'mma's nation is a confused invention because it erases a shared past. Bloody maneuvers to destabilize the British Raj were employed by the Muslims as well as the Hindus of colonial India in a joint effort to oust the oppressor. The composite culture constructed by the two communities was an inherent part of pre-colonial India as well, but is expunged by Tha'mma in her attempt to disseminate the unitary discourse of nationalism. Her militant nationalism does not evolve into critical nationalism: an awareness that unless national consciousness transforms into social consciousness, so-called "liberation" would merely be a continuation of imperialism (Said 323).

This point is illustrated by the partition of Tha'mma's ancestral house in pre-Partition Dhaka, another story that she relates to the narrator. As children she and her sister, Mayadebi, were part of an extended family. But after their grandfather died, their parents and their paternal uncle and his family grew apart. And "it did not take long for the quarrels to get worse" (122). Soon the situation became so unbearable that the two brothers decided to divide the house into two sections. This division vitiated the warmth and symmetry of the house so systemically that the divided portions had a grave-yard silence. The narrator recalls,

> They had all longed for the house to be divided when the quarrels were at their worst, but once it had actually happened and each family had moved into their own part of it, instead of the peace they had actually looked forward to, they found that a strange, eerie silence had descended on the house. It was never the same again after that; the life went out of it. It was worse for my grandmother than Mayadebi, for she could remember a time when it had been otherwise. She would often look across at her cousins on the other side and wonder about them, but so much bitterness lay between the two families now, that she could not bring herself to actually speak to them. (123)

The house across the divide is the antithesis to Tha'mma's house, and in order to entertain her sister, she fabricates the myth of an "upside-down" house, in which everything on the other side is the exact opposite to the way things are conducted in their house. The significance of that childish inversion was that as she grew older, Tha'mma began to believe the authenticity of her fabricated story, just as nationalists assert their correctness by believing that reversals occur across the border. I would argue that Tha'mma's nationalism is also colored by imperial rhetoric. The rhetoricians of imperialism after 1880 "deploy a language whose imagery of growth, fertility, and expansion, whose teleological structure of property and identity, whose ideological discrimination between 'us' and 'them' had already matured elsewhere—in fiction, political science, racial theory, travel writing" (Said 128). This ideological grounding and the language of cultural dominance are blatantly visible in Tha'mma's belief.[6] Ironically, the "Them" and the "Us" share a common lineage, just as the relatives in the upside-down house did. As Paul R. Brass observes about the view of nationalism that Tha'mma subscribes to,

> From the primordialist point of view, which was also the view of Muslim separatism, Hindus and Muslims constituted in pre-modern times distinct civilizations destined to develop into separate nations, once

political mobilization took place. The differences between the two cultures were so great that it was not conceivable that assimilation of the two could take place and that a single national culture could be created to which both would contribute. The contrary view is that the cultural and religious differences between Hindus and Muslims were not so great as to rule out the creation of either a composite national culture or at least a secular political union in which those aspects of group culture that could not be shared would be relegated to the private sphere. From this point of view, Muslim separatism was not preordained, but resulted from the conscious manipulation of selected symbols of Muslim identity by Muslim elite groups in economic and political competition with each other and with the elite among Hindus. (88)

Tha'mma's simplistic notion of nationalism as an alliance that is forged with people from the same religious, linguistic, cultural, and socio-economic background is seriously challenged by Ghosh. In addition to the confusion in her memory of the militant nationalist, we are also led to observe how the partition of the state of Bengal in 1947 into West Bengal and East Pakistan, the capital of which was Dhaka, leaves Tha'mma at a loss for words.

In a scene in which Tha'mma is worried about the prospect of filling out a disembarkation card upon her arrival in Bangladesh, the narrator captures a moment when the reality of her birth place, Dhaka, being the capital of an alien region finally sinks in:

It was not till many years later that I realized it had suddenly occurred to her then that she would have to fill in "Dhaka" as her place of birth on that form, and that the prospect of this had worried her in the same way that dirty schoolbooks worried her—because she liked things to be neat and in place—and at that moment she had not been able to quite understand how her place of birth had come to be so messily at odds with her nationality. (152)

Tha'mma, who had until that moment found comfort in the fixity of nationalism, is confronted with the illusory nature of that structure, and she finds herself compelled to recognize a glaring contradiction in the rigidity of that discourse. The realization that relentless violence and bloodshed cannot validate the "reality" of borders dawns on her.

This disturbing realization is further exacerbated when Mayadebi, whose husband has been made Counselor in the deputy high commission there, invites Tha'mma to Dhaka. At first, she decides this visit will be a welcome opportunity. It would enable her to try to persuade her paternal uncle, who still lives in their ancestral house there but is now afflicted with senility, to "return" to India. Although her uncle had never lived anywhere else but Dhaka, she is inspired to take him "home" to India because the tenet of nationalism to which she subscribes circumscribes people with the same religious and national identity both psychologically and physically. Ironically, her uncle's, Jethamoshai's, only claim to an Indian identity is the religion he was born into, Hinduism. Other than that, geographically and physically he is moored to that part of the country which after 1947 became Pakistani territory. As he had once told his sons before they migrated to India, "I don't believe in India—Shindia. As for me, I was born here, and I'll die here" (216).

Just before flying to Dhaka, Tha'mma asks her son, the narrator's father, if "she would be able to see the border between India and East Pakistan from the plane." When her son mockingly asks if she thinks the border is "a long black line with green on one side and scarlet on the other, like it was in the school atlas," her deeply entrenched idea of cartographical divisions is rendered inarticulate (151). She inadvertently challenges her own cherished ideology of nationalism:

> But if there aren't any trenches or anything, how are people to know? I mean, where's the difference then? And if there's no difference both sides will be the same; it'll be just like it was before, when we used to catch a train in Dhaka and get off in Calcutta the next day without anyone stopping us. What was it all for then—partition and all the killing and everything—if there isn't something in between? (151)

Because of the tremendous physical changes in the country, Tha'mma is not even able to recognize Dhaka once she gets there, and she cannot sustain her fanatical view of nationalism, according to which the other side is an inverted version of the true world. On entering that portion of their ancestral house that was at one time occupied by their uncle and his family, Tha'mma and Mayadebi cry tears of joy at the epiphany that "Nothing is upside down" (212).

In this instance, the unhistoricized historiography that is manifested in personal memory reveals the fictive nature of official historiography. The nation is exposed as "an imagined political community," because, as Benedict Anderson points out, "members of even the smallest nation will never know most of their fellow members, meet them, or even hear of them, yet in the minds of each lives the image of their communion" (15). At least for this moment, it is Tha'mma's personal memory of history that empowers her to shake off the yoke of the official versions of history. This attempt to recollect the minutiae of her childhood in Dhaka is lauded by the narrator, who observes that "people like my grandmother, who have no home but in memory, learn to be very skilled in the art of recollection" (194). Still, Tha'mma's sense of filial duty motivates her to take their senile uncle back with them to India. When she goes to their ramshackle mansion with Mayadebi, Tridib, his brother, Robi, and May to persuade Jethamoshai to accompany them, she ends up succeeding in her endeavor, but at a calamitous price.

While walking toward their car, they notice that it has been surrounded by an intemperate mob: "There were dozens of them stretched all the way across the road. They had lit a fire in the middle of the road, with a few broken chairs and bits of wood. Some of them were squatting around the fire, others were leaning against the lamp-posts and the shop-fronts" (217). For his heroic effort to rescue their chauffer and security guard, who are in the midst of the scavenging mob, Tridib is mercilessly lynched and dies a death that terrorizes the petrified witnesses for the rest of their remaining days. Tha'mma remains a mute spectator to the merciless murder of Tridib by the unruly mob.

In this scene, Ghosh graphically portrays the heightened impetuousness and insanity that the anonymity of the mob brings out in its constituents. The jarring sounds of the blustering rhetoric of hate and destruction fill the air and engender a mass hysteria that seems to legitimize an unquenchable thirst for blood. It is the fictiveness of the sense of community and the flaunting of its signifiers, national flags, national anthems, and jingoism that underwrite the abstract affirmation of nationalist ideology. Time and again, the novel highlights the fictive nature of history. This terrifying incident unravels the realm woven by Tha'mma's memory of history and hauls her back into the cell of official historiography. Tridib's death casts her into the mold of the avenger, and she contributes to the fund for the 1965 war with Pakistan by donating a gold chain that had been given to her by her husband. In her frenzy, she tells the narrator of her unwavering commitment to eliminate the monstrous "they" so "we" and posterity could breathe in an atmosphere that had been cleansed of noxious elements: "I gave it to the fund for the war. For your sake, for your freedom. We have to kill them before they kill us; we have to wipe them out" (237).

During the narrator's subsequent inquiry regarding the riots of 1964 at the Teen Murti House Library in New Delhi, he discovers that the riots that were a looming presence in his life found negligible mention in the newspapers and chronicles of that time. His research is a rude awakening because he discovers that "[b]y the end of January 1964 the riots had faded away from the pages of the newspapers, disappeared from the collective imagination of 'responsible' opinion, vanished, without leaving a trace in the histories and bookshelves" (230). This startling discovery reveals that history is not an "objective" record of events but, on the contrary, a fabrication wrought by ideological state apparatuses. The narrator astutely points out that the failure to report on the 1964 riots was an act of deliberate and culpable erasure: "they must have known. . . . All the canny journalists; everybody must have known in some voiceless part of themselves-for events on that scale cannot happen without portents. If they knew, why couldn't they speak of it[?]" (227). On the other hand, other events that occurred that year, such as "the Congress conference," "the impending split in the Communist party," and "wars and revolutions," were given thorough coverage (228).

Because of the minimal coverage of the riots, the narrator's friend, Malik, draws the inference that they must have been a "local thing. . . . Hardly comparable to a war" (221). The refutation of this inference and the exposure of these abysmal lacunae in history come when the narrator discovers, to his chagrin, that the eruption of communal riots in Dhaka was simultaneous with the eruption of political frenzy in Calcutta and with political and communal tension in Kashmir that reverberated in Pakistan. The narrator informs us that in December 1963, an ancient relic was stolen from a mosque in Kashmir, which incited tempestuous reactions: "there were some incidents of rioting and a curfew was declared by the authorities" (225). The repercussions of this incident were so widespread that they shook the foundations not just of the picturesque valley but also of neighboring Pakistan: "In Pakistan there were meetings and demonstrations in towns and cities in both wings of the country" (226). Despite the seismic effect of these events that shook the entire subcontinent, the narrator finds that the newspapers had chosen to bury historical facts by maintaining a stony silence about the events of December 1963 and 1964: "I found that there was not the slightest reference to any trouble in East Pakistan, and the barest mention of the events in Kashmir" (227).

It is at this point that he recalls that the day Tridib was killed by the rioters in Dhaka, he had fleetingly seen the horrendous riots in Calcutta through the windows of his school bus: "I could not have perceived that there was something more than an incidental connection between those events of which I had a brief glimpse from the windows of that bus, in Calcutta, and those other events in Dhaka, simply because Dhaka was in another country" (219). The narrator's revealing discovery of the simultaneity of events in Dhaka and Calcutta and the rumbling in East Pakistan of the thunder in Kashmir bears testimony to the vital importance of a transnational imagination. This imagination is cognizant of the irony that the moment of national separation never actually takes place.

The narrator articulates this paradox when he recalls the 1964 riots in Calcutta and Dhaka that left an indelible mark on his family. Referring to the role played by nationalist parties in the Partition of the subcontinent, the narrator queries,

> What had they felt, I wondered, when they discovered that they had created not a separation, but a yet-undiscovered irony—the irony that killed Tridib: the simple fact that there had never been a moment in the four-thousand-year-old history of that map, when the places we know as Calcutta and Dhaka were more closely bound together . . . So closely that I, in Calcutta, had only to look into the mirror to be in Dhaka; when each city was the inverted image of the other, locked into an irreversible symmetry by the line that was to set us free—our looking-glass border. (233)

This articulation of the supplementary and unstable structure of nation-states is a profound deconstruction of the notion of an "originary" source of identity. The narrator identifies a contradiction in the concept of the fixity of nationalist ideology, because in order to provide a point of origin, which organizes the stability of the structure, subjectivity needs to be a part of the structure as well as of the periphery. So the similarity in the emotions evoked by communal and religious affiliations on the two sides of the border renders the inclusion/exclusion dichotomy incoherent, making riots and mobs fit emblems of its logic.

I contend that in rejecting the meta-identity of nationalism, Ghosh seems to privilege a universalism that has been rejected for its hegemonic and manipulative power by many postcolonial scholars. By doing so, he also might appear to belittle nationalist struggles of dispossessed peoples in battling communities that need to assert themselves. Universalism is as shaky and fluid an idea as nationalism and is too utopian to provide a genuine solution to the actual problems bred by nationalism. Universalism has often been identified with imperialist ideologies that purport to support a "civilizing mission" that creates a totalizing or homogenizing center.

Helen Tiffin comments about the universalist criteria that negate the historical and sociocultural specificities of a people by insisting that life in a Third-World country is similar to life in a metropolitan center because of the essential camaraderie of mankind, "[A]n orthodoxy has developed which dismisses realist writers as inherently inferior to those with more overtly metaphysical interests" (28). Universalist critics prefer writers who undermine the local and the specific. According to Arun Mukherjee, "The universalist critic, armed with his ready-made categories of narrative technique, symbolic pat-

terns, motifs such as journey or quest, bildungsroman, pastoral, etc., overlooks the formal complexities that arise when a work openly or cryptically
utilizes the collectively shared knowledge and experiences of a society: experience of colonialism, legends of heroes and villains, deeply held belief systems, rhetorical pronouncements of local elite such as politicians,
businessmen and movie stars and so on" (21). In such situations, the "universal" circumvents the need to see the alien and refuses to deal with a world
that has been radically transformed by struggle.

In a world that has been sinking further into the morass of political
unaccountability and cultural repression after the gut-wrenching events of
September 11, 2001; the fizzling out of the fragile Peace Pact in Palestine in
2003; the installation of putatively de jure regimes in Afghanistan and Iraq,
and the unspeakable degradations the populaces of those countries were subjected to; the Hindutva movement in India, with its privileging the idea of
an ethnically pure Hindu nation, neither a single theoretical compartment
nor a celebratory discourse of hybridity is adequate to frame multiple subjectivities and histories. The communal riots in the Indian state of Gujarat that
occurred in 2002 divided the state along religious lines causing such irreparable damage that its seismic tremors continue to destabilize other regions of
the Indian subcontinent, kindling Muslim/Hindu antipathy in Kashmir and
Bombay as recently as August 2003. Unfortunately, such recurrences of bigotry are funded by transnational communities in their desire to return to an
idealized distant past.[7] Despite its theoretical aversion to contemporary cultural nationalisms, postcolonialism is appropriated by such movements.
These cultural nationalisms are produced by transnational communities
from a distance and are the consequence of nostalgic imaginings, negating
Ghosh's utopian universalism.

Chapter Five
Places and the Politics of Identity in Desai's *In Custody*

> My writing is an effort to discover, underline and convey the significance
> of things. I must seize upon that incomplete and seemingly meaningless
> mass of reality around me and try and discover its significance by plung-
> ing below the surface and plumbing the depths, then illuminating those
> depths till they become more lucid, brilliant and inexplicable reflections
> of the visible world. (Desai, "Replies to the Questionnaire" 5)

As I explained in the previous chapter, the nation-states of India and Pakistan were forged by the heart-rending separateness of "Hindus" and "Muslims." In the aftermath of Independence and Partition, administrative fiats
strengthened the religious divide. For instance, in September 1947, the government of India established the Military Evacuation Organization to get
Hindus and Sikhs out of Pakistan in an organized and efficient fashion (Rao
15). I argue that this severance politicized not just religious identities but linguistic identities as well. So the Urdu poet Nur Shahjenabadi in Anita Desai's
In Custody berates the timid Hindi lecturer, Deven, "Forgotten your Urdu?
Forgotten my verse?," and mockingly tells him to remain shrouded in the
"safe, simple Hindi language, safe comfortable ideas of cow worship and
caste . . ." (55).

In this chapter, by looking at Anita Desai's novel, *In Custody*, I explore
the constitutive elements of the post-Independence sense of the nation. I
argue that Desai's novel delineates the internal hierarchies entrenched by
nationalism in relation to an array of matters: political power, ethnicity, religion, religious prejudice, and other problems permeating the Indian subcontinent. It is at that moment in the new-born nation that Muslims discover
what it is never to qualify as the norm. I also argue that the world of Urdu

literature is portrayed as the domain of male friendships in which the male narrator deifies the Urdu poet, Nur, and is leery of the poet's talented wife, Imtiaz, whose attempts to wax eloquent are perceived as an incursion into a carefully guarded male domain. Desai deploys Deven's suspicion of Imtiaz and the docility of his wife, Sarla, to portray and subtly critique the objectification of the "Third-World Woman" as the repository of a pre-colonial cultural essence. I demonstrate the production of women not as a universal category but as a socioeconomic and political group within a particular local context.[1]

In Custody highlights the impoverishment of the cultural and linguistic forms of Muslim identity in post-1947 India, as when one of Nur Shahjen-abadi's cronies says, "Urdu is supposed to have died, in 1947. What you see in the universities—in some of the universities, a few of them only—is its ghost, wrapped in a shroud" (56). In reference to the complicity of the Congress leadership in giving preference to Hindi in postcolonial India, the Urdu poet Nur Shahjenabadi declares in the novel, "Those Congress-wallahs have set up Hindi on top as our ruler" (42).

As Prabhu S. Guptara reminds the student of Indian history, the recognition of English and Hindi by the Constitution of independent India as the nation's two official languages enabled Hindi to make "significant strides, and the number of publications has been growing steadily" (24). The nation and nationalism that were defined by the politics of the Partition need to be analyzed in order to account for the volcanic eruptions caused by this horrific event.

For instance, an illustrious Urdu poet, Faiz Ahmad Faiz, writes his account of the fear, sense of loss, and bewilderment that followed in the wake of the "The Dawn of Freedom (August 1947)." In this rendition, Faiz's arduous endeavor to articulate his outrage at "the terrible rampant lie" and the audacious attempt of the nationalist leadership to provide a rationalization for it is well grounded:

> Now listen to the terrible rampant lie: Light has forever been severed
> from the Dark; our feet, it is heard, are now one with their goal. See our
> leaders polish their manner clean of our suffering: Indeed we must con-
> fess only to bliss; we must surrender any utterance for the Beloved—all
> yearning is outlawed. (II.16–21)

In this pain-filled account of the emotional depletion and psychological decrepitude that were the "collateral damages" of the decolonization of India and its subsequent geographical division, Faiz makes an attempt to expose, and thus reject, the nationalist panacea. This panacea, which was designed to lead

the physically defaced and psychically mangled communities to resign themselves to an incomprehensible transformation, is deconstructed by the poet.

Beyond the rifts that were first brought to the surface in the Indian
subcontinent in 1947, the forces of communal violence, and fundamentalism continue to wield their power with unabated vigor. In the context of
these historical ruptures, poems such as the one by Faiz and similar narratives
describe the experience of the disenfranchised Muslims and Hindus, who
were uprooted during the Partition, and require the reader to consider their
experiences. The insistence on a nationalist rhetoric that prevents a nation
from retrieving and performing a critical examination of its culture, social
customs, its gender divisions is rendered more urgent by such narratives.

In Desai's novel, the narrator, Deven, strives assiduously to fabricate a
mythic realm within which to escape constructing new dimensions of cultural
possibility. Jasbir Jain, however, delineates the difficulty involved in clinging to
the world of imagination and art in the face of petty realities that Deven aspires
to elude: "Life all around seems determined to outcrowd art. Deven in his struggle for daily survival, has shelved his artistic involvements and concerns" (106).
In order to earn sustenance to support his spouse, Sarla, and child, the narrator
has put his passion for Urdu literature on the back burner and opted to teach
Hindi literature as a lecturer at a small college in the Indian town of Mirpore.
Deven's choice of the field of Hindi literature is an alienating experience because
he has no discernible interest in the subject. He is a talented poet whose imagination has been stimulated by Urdu poetry.

Thus, when Deven is given the welcome chance of conducting an
interview with Nur Shahjehanabadi, a renowned and aging Urdu poet, his
excitement knows no bounds because this promises deliverance from a prosaic and unstimulating world. The opportunity to interview Nur knocks on
his door when his friend Murad, who is the editor of a moribund Urdu journal, *Awaaz* (Voice), contemplates putting together a compilation of the
priceless works of the illustrious Urdu poets of yore. Murad claims that he
aspires to shoulder the responsibility of bolstering "the glorious tradition of
Urdu poetry," because Hindi, as he derogatorily puts it, is the "language of
peasants. The language that is raised on radishes and potatoes." Murad goes
into a rhapsody about the regal past of Urdu, "language of the court in days
of royalty" (15). In addition, for the narrator Nur evokes fond memories of a
mythicized past because his father was an ardent admirer of the poet's work
and recited it with an incomparable verve: "[Deven] went on reciting that
great poem of Nur's that his father had loved to recite and that he still read,
ceremoniously, whenever he felt sad or nostalgic and thought of his father
and his early childhood and all that he had lost" (44).

But in post-colonial and post-Partition India, Urdu finds itself abandoned by its wealthy and regal patrons of the pre-Partition era, who are reeling under the disorienting effects of geographical dislocation. In the era of the decrepitude of the glorious traditions of the Urdu language, there is "no palace for it to live in the style to which it is accustomed, no emperors and nawabs to act as its patrons" (15). The language of regal courts is not yet acclimated to petty realities. So the dethroning of Urdu literature and poetry has left a lecturer like Deven with no alternative but to write Urdu in his spare time. He perceives his responsibilities toward his family and his job as a Hindi lecturer as "heaps of rubbish" that thwart the strides he seeks to make toward literary fame and glory.

The narrator's sense of sterility is accentuated by the aridity and stagnation of Mirpore, which offers no stimulation to an aspiring artist. Mirpore is a "strip of no-man's land that lies around a prison threatening in its desolation" (24). Surprisingly, Deven is tormented by the thought of being unable to escape the incarceration not only of "the walled courtyard" in Mirpore, but his purposeless existence in "the walled city" of Delhi while working on the project for the Urdu journal, *Awaaz:* "He was thinking that the great city was no different from his own small town and that the dissimilarity lay only in scale: this was certainly larger, noisier, more crowded and chaotic, but that was all, and it was the scale and not the unfamiliarity that made him feel so small, weak and inadequate" (15).

Historically, the Partition of 1947 did fragment the writing community by redistributing its members into two separate territorial nations. One of the significant consequences of the Partition was the migration of Urdu writers of Muslim origin to Pakistan. So the chime of Independence was, as Aijaz Ahmad eloquently puts it, "experienced in the whole range of Urdu literature of the period not in the celebratory mode but as a defeat, a disorientation, a diaspora" (*Lineages* 118). As Deven explains, Urdu literature "had become doomed the day the Muslims departed across the newly drawn border of the new country of Pakistan" (16). This is one of the unfortunate calamities of India's historical past whose religio-cultural tensions continue today to sharpen divisions along communal lines in the country. As Desai writes of one of the manifestations of communal tensions in the town of Mirpore, "For a while tension was high, the newspapers—both in Hindi and Urdu—were filled with guarded reports and fulsome editorials on India's secularity while overnight newssheets appeared with less guarded reports laced with threats and accusations" (21). In independent India, the violent backlash after the rout of British colonialism and the exploitation of divided communal sentiments by political and religious leaders had evoked divisive militancy in the garb of patriotism.

In the modern world, religious and cultural differences are deliberately fostered by many nation-states in their efforts to construct homogenous subjects of state. So Chandra Chatterjee tells the reader about the redefinition of Hinduism in pre-Independence India, which was engendered in reaction to colonial rule in India and also in reaction to the challenge to the nation by ethnic and religious groups in post-Independence democratic and secular India:

> It is well known that the term Hindu is a broad-based loose definition used by the Muslim invaders for those living in India who were not the followers of Islam. This included all the tribals and the communities from the remote corners of the country even when they followed distinct forms of worship, quite different from Aryan Hinduism. . . . But the various communal uprisings based on religion are forcing the Hindus to uphold their identity and lean towards it with self-consciousness unknown in the last two centuries.

> However, democracy in India is itself protest-ridden. The ethnic and religious minorities protest against the singular definition of "nation." The politically marginalized groups protest against inadequate representation in government policies. Numerous insurgencies all over the country relate their revolts to wars for independence at the sub-national level which the dominant national ideology has been unable to either outwit or neutralize. (7–8)

Sentiments of regional separatism, for example, incited the masses in the south Indian state of Tamil Nadu and in the north Indian state of Kashmir aided by religious fervor within a purportedly secular framework. In both Tamil Nadu and Kashmir the issue of a separate identity to counter internal colonialism has resurfaced in contemporary times with an unparalleled ferocity.

So Deven's spellbound and enthralled response to the poet, when he is finally summoned into his presence, isn't surprising. Nur's imperious beckoning holds the allure of religion and myth for the protagonist:

> It was to him as if God had leaned over a cloud and called for him to come up, and angels might have been drawing him up these ancient splintered stairs to meet the deity. This, surely, was the summons he had been waiting for all these empty years. He had never conceived of a summons expressed in a voice so leonine . . . a voice that could grasp him, as it were, by the roots of his hair and haul him up from the level on which he existed—mean, disordered and hopeless—into another, higher sphere. Another realm it would surely be if his god dwelt there, the domain of poetry, beauty and illumination. (39–40)

Deven's predilection for Urdu is the author's recognition of a literary form that contests any attempt to homogenize Indian culture. Similarly, it also opposes the privileging of Hindi in official and educational institutions. I would suggest that the recognition of this subcontinental heritage also allows Desai to redefine the dominant self-image of Indian culture within post-colonial India, which perpetuates the domination of the high-caste north Indian Hindus over those whom they consider to be descendants of the Afghan and Moghul invaders and of inferior south Indian origin. Desai deconstructs this self-image by including voices that present alternative social realities.

To conduct his interview with Nur, who spends almost all his waking moments in the garret of his house, Deven ascends the stairs feeling as though he is "sloughing off and casting away the meanness and dross" of his humdrum life. The poet's house is located in a labyrinthine area, Chandini Chowk, which is inhabited by a menagerie of wastrels: "If it had not been for the color and the noise, Chandini Chowk might have been a bazaar encountered in a nightmare; it was so like a maze from which he could find no exit. The heat and the crowds pressed down from above and all sides, solid and suffocating as sleep" (36). Yet Deven is so enthralled by his anticipated meeting with the poet that at first he fails to notice the pathetic surroundings: the broken bike, the dripping tap, and the dusty stairs. However, once Deven enters the poet's room, the shabbiness, chaos, and disorder are discomfiting, and he is unable to turn a blind eye to the literal and metaphorical debris surrounding his mythicized idol.

This is a moment of psychological crisis for the narrator, who had found refuge in Nur's verse because it "placed frightening and inexplicable experiences like time and death at a point where they could be seen and studied, in safety" (54). As S. Indira observes, "the darkness of Nur's house suggests that his creative vision is gone into eclipse and that his entire life is darkened now with vices and mediocrity" (155). This experience generates an ideological and intellectual rift between Deven's grandiose visions of art and poetry and the distressing reality of Nur's existence. Deven's imaginary world and the delusions of grandeur he nurtures in it are further dispelled when the poet declares in a voice of certitude that Urdu poetry is dead: "How can there be Urdu poetry when there is no Urdu language left? . . . The defeat of the Moghuls by the British threw a noose over its head, and the defeat of the British by the Hindi-wallahs tightened it" (42). As Nur's despairing statement indicates, the decay of the Urdu language and its literature and culture in post-Partition India is an effect of the imposition of the singular definition of nation against which ethnic and religious minorities continue to protest in present-day India.

Deven's poignant realization of the poet's excruciatingly painful, degrading, and petty disease, piles, brings him to recognize that he is unable to reconcile the pettiness of Nur's physical existence with the immensity of his verse. He asks himself, "In taking Nur's art into his hands, did he have to gather up the stained, soiled, discolored, and odorous rags of his life as well?" (158). The pedestal on which he had placed the poet gets chipped even more when he becomes cognizant of Nur's depraved dependence on the obsequiousness of his hangers-on. These hangers-on are a bunch of wastrels who have a spiritually parasitic relationship with the poet and sponge off his meager resources: "It was clear to Deven that these louts, these lafangas of the bazaar world—shopkeepers, clerks, bookies and unemployed parasites—lived out the fantasy of being poets, artists and bohemians here on Nur's terrace, in Nur's company" (50). Deven had hoped that forging a rapport with his hero would empower him to repress the feelings of unworthiness and insecurity born of his work in the study of Hindi literature, which did not allow him to inhabit a language that would enrich him with a meaningful existence. Now, however, his romantic perception of art and life is eroded. There is also a suggestion here that Deven's inability to recognize the material pressures of his time has potentially made him just another parasite fantasizing about being an Urdu poet.

The revelation that assuming responsibility for the poet's lofty and sublime poetry would include satiating the demands of his squabbling wives and his brazen toadies shakes Deven's sense of commitment to his project. Deven's fierce loathing of these unpleasant external realities prods him to try to cast them into oblivion, but the poet perceives his interviewer's desire and inquires during one of their recording sessions: "Has this dilemma come to you too then? This sifting and selecting from the debris of our lives? It can't be done my friend, it can't be done, I learnt that long ago" (167).

It is apropos that this recording session is conducted in the run-down brothel in which the poet's second wife, Imtiaz Begum, was an acclaimed nautch girl. Nur's point that the world of cultural depletion, dislocation, and impoverishment cannot be separated from that of exalted poetry, romance, and alluring myth seems to be endorsed by Desai, who invests the narrator with the authority to be the custodian of Nur's oeuvre but acknowledges that the world of everyday reality cannot be ignored. The relegation of Urdu poetry to an edifice of crumbling decadence and the ennobling of a nautch girl to the keeper of the material and spiritual dimensions of the poet's home blurs the distinction between the poetic and the prosaic. This insistence on

the lack of dogmatism negates any tendency to theorize a cultural self-definition at the cost of voices that may present a different side of the same picture.

However, despite Deven's inexorable devotion to and protective concern for Nur's poetry, he remains unwilling to extend that concern to the
poet's two wives. The poet's second wife, Imtiaz Begum, is described as an
"apparition of fury and vengeance" (58). Her picture is etched in the narrator's memory as the harridan with "spittle-flecked red lips which had parted
to scream abuse at the poet" (64). For Deven, the poet's wives like his own
wife are representatives of petty and degrading detail, in contrast to the presumed sublimity of Urdu poetry. He is unable to imagine a form of artistic
and social agency in which such sterile aspects of the culture are rendered
defunct.

But I would argue that Imtiaz rescues the term "Indian Woman" from
the homogenizing power of the culture industry and "lays bare the travesty
of unifying women in India under any single category" (Chatterjee 95).
Imtiaz Begum deplores the depraved state into which her husband has sunk
and makes no bones about loathing the unglamorous life that she is forced to
live with Nur. Seeing him sink into the dregs of sickness and despair, a flus-
tered Imtiaz Begum cries out, "See what he's done in my room? Am I to
stand for this in my room, in my house? Did he marry me to make me live in
a pigsty with him?" (60). Her cacophonous reaction to Nur's despondency is
augmented because she, unlike the poet's illiterate first wife, Safiya Begum, is
an admirer of the baroque quality of his verse and is a budding poetess who
strives to emulate his elegance and floridity. Being unconcerned about the
reaction evoked by her former status as a courtesan, Imtiaz Begum covets the
position of Nur's "intellectual companion." She claims, "Yet there must have
been some natural gift if Nur Sahib himself was impressed by my early verse.
It is the reason he married me in his old age, to have at his side an intellectual
companion of the kind he did not have in his first marriage" (196). Imtiaz's
readiness to play the role of Nur's "intellectual companion" runs contrary to
the traditional representation of the native woman as a silent symbol of
nationhood. But her poetic sublimity is compromised by her egoism that
leads her to present images from Nur's well-known poems as her own in her
recitals.

As opposed to Imtiaz, the narrator's wife, Sarla, is a middle-class house-
wife who is embittered by thwarted dreams and aspirations. She is portrayed
as a traditional woman who has never had the audacity either to appreciate
art with sensitivity and perceptiveness or to develop her own intellect.
Rather, the hopes that she has nurtured are of material plenitude provided by
a doting householder: a luxury vehicle, a "gleaming refrigerator," and a "tele-

phone placed on a lacy doily" so she can indulge herself by calling her friends "to invite them to see a picture show with her and her husband," whose uxoriousness would be overwhelming (68). But these dreams have been dashed because of her academic husband's inability to provide for her. Sarla accepts her life of mediocrity with the resignation and endurance of a mute victim. Although Deven makes an earnest attempt to sympathize with the plight his wife is in, her surly fortitude doesn't fill the abyss that separates him from Sarla:

> He understood because like her, he had been defeated too; like her, he was a victim. . . . A victim does not look to help from another victim; he looks for a redeemer. (68)

Deven can immerse himself in the grandeur and sublimity of poetry in order to dwell in the realm of glory, fantasy, and masculinity. But Sarla is doomed to be miserable and bear the pangs of "the thwarting of her aspirations," which "had cut two dark furrows from the corners of her nostrils to the corners of her mouth" (68).

The portrayal of Sarla clearly illustrates that nationalist discourse is not a discourse by women and remains trapped within its edifice of debilitating essentialisms. Sarla is unable to rebel against the traditional Hindu philosophy of detachment from life and resignation to whatever the future has in store. Similarly, Imtiaz Begum's attempt to assert an individuality that would enable her to be recognized as a poetess in her own right is met with disdain by her husband's admirers and cronies. In contemporary Indian society, as in Desai's 1984 novel, the question of the role of women in the nationalist scenario remains a vexed one. As Ann McClintock observes about the role of the subaltern woman in "Third-World" societies, "Excluded from direct action as national citizens, women are subsumed symbolically into the national body politic as its boundary and metaphoric limit" (345). For instance, the ruling political party in India, the Bharatiya Janata Party (BJP) has a woman's wing that claims that the image of woman as powerful mother underlines economic independence for women and reinforces her strength and courage of conviction to sacrifice for the family. The BJP vociferously campaigns for quotas for women in parliament and the judiciary. The women members of this political party argue that they could never identify the modern Indian woman with the liberated woman of the Western world. On the contrary, they campaign for reverting to a mythic past where women were putatively equals in society. In doing so, the women's wing of the BJP makes an ardent attempt to reconstruct history in order to inspire the kind of nationalism that present-day politics requires. Chatterjee tells us about the measures such politics inspires in contemporary Indian society:

> From the 1990s, through a government order, 30% of jobs in the government were reserved for women. But when the same reservation was demanded in Parliament in the form of the Women's Reservation Bill, various political parties saw to it that the issue was not easily entered for debate. Though women form half of India's total population their strength in the Lower House [of Parliament] is about 43 in a total of more than 500 members. (105)

The argument that is made is that such quotas will not benefit the backward castes, so only women belonging to those groups should avail themselves of this quota. These subdivisions caused by categorizing women along caste and religious lines perpetuate divisive politics.

In effect, the native woman is constructed as a trough within which male aspirations are nurtured, and the most barbaric acts are justified as means to restore the lost dignity of the "women." The story of the partition of India in 1947 into two separate nation-states, India and Pakistan, is replete with instances of fathers slaughtering their daughters in order to prevent them from being violated by the enemy; women resorting to mass suicide to preserve the "honor" of the community; and women who were "dishonored" being ruthlessly shunned by their families.[2]

As recently as 2002, the Indian state of Gujarat was ransacked by communal violence and hatred. One of the ramifications of the fury was the gruesome rape and murder of Muslim women by Hindu perpetrators. This bestiality was avenged by the Muslim community by the brutal violation of a group of Hindu women. The putative purpose of the retaliatory act was the restoration of dignity to the Hindu community, the logic being that a violent act against a defenseless female is tantamount to the castration of her male protector. Within hours of the outrage committed by the Muslim perpetrators in Gujarat, three fanatical Hindu organizations, the Vishwa Hindu Parishad, the Bajrang Dal, and the Rashtriya Samaj Sevak (RSS), set

> into motion a meticulously planned pogrom against the Muslim community. Press reports put the number of dead just over 800. Human rights organizations have said it is closer to 2,000. As many as 100,000 people, driven from their homes, now live in refugee camps. Women were stripped and gang-raped, and parents were bludgeoned to death in front of their children. In Ahmadabad, the former capital of Gujarat and the second-largest city in the state, the tomb of Wali Gujarati, the

founder of the modern Urdu poem, was demolished and paved over in the course of a night. The tomb of the musician Ustad Faiyaz Khan was desecrated. . . . The leaders of the mob had computer-generated lists marking out Muslim homes, shops and businesses. . . . Hundreds of RSS shakhas across the country (shakha literally means 'branch,' and RSS shakhas are 'educational' cells) have been indoctrinating thousands of children and young people, stunting their minds with religious hatred and falsified history, including unfactual or wildly exaggerated accounts of the rape and pillaging of Hindu women and Hindu temples by Muslim rulers in the precolonial period. (Roy 17–18)

Reinforcing this logic, in Hindu nationalist rhetoric the equation of the sanctity of the native female to the motherland has in recent days become more forceful. Why is gender violence such a consistent feature of the communal riots that spasmodically grip India? If a woman's body belongs not to herself but to her community, then the violation of that body purportedly signifies an attack upon the honor (izzat) of the whole community.[3]

Such irrational acts do occur and bear testimony to the intersecting notions of nation, family, and community. The horrific stories of women that are in most instances attributed to folklore underscore the complicity of official and nationalist historiography in perpetuating these notions. I might add that the feminization of the "homeland" as the "motherland" for which nationalists are willing to lay down their lives serves, in effect, to preserve the native women in pristine retardation.

In her novels, Desai foregrounds powerful feminist trends in the "Third-World." Most of her works delve into the construction of the "Third-World Woman," who is in search of an identity other than the one imposed on her by the nationalist movements and literatures of postcolonial India. As Leela Gandhi points out in her refreshing analysis of the place that native Indian women occupy in nationalist discourse, the ideal of "authentic" Indian womanhood was bolstered in order to demonize Western women. As opposed to the Western "memsahib," the Indian woman was endowed with goddess-like attributes as the keeper of home and hearth. Gandhi is quick to point out that "the nation authenticates its distinct cultural identity through its women" (96). Nationalist discourse creates the dichotomy of the inner/outer in order to make the sanctity of the inviolable inner domain look traditional. Nationalist writers assert that as long as the inner or spiritual distinctiveness of the culture is retained, a postcolonial nation can make the required adjustments in order to cope with a modern material world without losing its essential identity. The result, however, is not the orderly process of modernization but rather the continued immisera-

tion of women. For instance, although Sarla's household is teetering under
the pressures of modern society with all its drastic changes in science, technology, and cultural and political institutions, her protests are muted. She
continues to live subserviently in a union of sexual and material frustration.
In one scene, Sarla expresses resentment by isolating herself from the immediate surroundings in the benign detachment of herself "from the doorpost
. . . , holding the fold of her sari firmly over her head as if she were in mourn-
ing or at a religious ceremony" (66). But in the process of hankering after
solitude and withdrawal from the world, Sarla is guilty of not "engaging
more effectively with the politics of affiliation, and the currently calamitous
dispensations of power" (McClintock 396).

     But I argue that in post-Independence India, in which the trumpets of
nationalism are blaring, Sarla struggles to conform to the nationalist dogma,
according to which the quintessence of the home must remain uncontaminated by the vile pursuits of the material world, with its purity embodied by
the woman (Karamcheti 127). She is a passive victim who represents chastity
and honor. Consider Gayatri Chakravorty Spivak's delineation of the contexts in which the politics of representation renders mute the figure of the
"Third-World woman":

> Between patriarchy and imperialism, subject-constitution and object-
> formation, the figure of the woman disappears, not into a pristine noth-
> ingness, but a violent shuttling which is the displaced figuration of the
> "third-world woman" caught between tradition and modernization.
> (*Critique* 765)

The discourse disseminated by imperialism and that disseminated by nationalism do not allow the "Third-World woman" to speak for herself. The com-
peting discourses that speak through her render the native woman incapable
of exercising agency. Sarla in her helplessness and Deven in his attitude
toward Nur's wives are both rendered incapable of liberating themselves from
the myths of the golden age of pre- and post-colonial India.

     So Imtiaz's ambitions threaten to confound the normative structure.
The postcolonial scholar Partha Chatterjee makes an interesting observation
regarding this construct: the role of woman as goddess or mother binds her
to a form of subordination that is the exercise of dominance without hegemony (130). In other words, in the present socio-political set up, the image
of the Indian Woman as the impregnable barrier against the perversion of
Indian values is an ideal which incarcerates her. The iconization of woman as
goddess-mother circumscribes her movement within society. Women who

choose to break the mold created by patriarchy are denied even the meager freedom that the domestic image has bestowed and are left no choice but to resort to their own devices. For example, in *In Custody* Imtiaz accuses the narrator of having been complicit in leaving her no choice but to display herself to generous male patrons of the arts of pleasure, love, and sexuality:

> Are you not guilty of assuming that because you are a male, you have a right to brains, talent, reputation and achievement, while I, because I was born female, am condemned to find what satisfaction I can in being maligned, mocked, ignored and neglected? Is it not you who has made me play the role of the loose woman in gaudy garments by refusing to take my work seriously and giving me just that much regard that you would extend to even a failure in the arts as long as the artist was male? (196)

Despite the encouragement of women's education in post-Partition India, the womanly virtues of devotion, submission, chastity, and patience are still viewed as the social forms that tradition inculcates in women. Nationalist discourse creates a framework that confers upon women the pre-lapsarian mythological status of a selfless, asexual, benevolent, and maternal entity. As U. Chakrabarty theorizes, because the edifice of national culture was propped up by ideals of purity, selfless love, and sacrifice, the decapacitation of women was the result (143). Imtiaz realizes that a woman who does not conform to that construct is in the irreparable position of a fallen seductress, because the very definition of nationhood has been made contingent upon the male recognition of her identity. But the loneliness of the mythic realm and the self-abnegation that it demands are values that need to be renounced to allow the subject to work through the past in order to construct new dimensions of cultural possibility. So, too, does Deven have to renounce his mythic realm of pure Urdu literature.

The ordinary, the sordid, and the humdrum of the present can never be separated from the mythic retreat into the realm of glory and fable, here symbolized by the past. In recognition of this fact, Desai's Deven finally comprehends that the man he has forged an alliance with is not an anthropomorphized deity but a person who is bogged down by marital, parental, social, and communal relations that oblige him to observe vacuous rituals for the sake of convention, just as he himself is obliged to do. So after accepting the gift of Nur Shahjenabadi's oeuvre from the poet, Deven revels in rapturous delight, but "he turned back. He walked up the path. Soon the sun would be up and blazing. The day would begin, with its calamities. They would flash out of the sky and cut him down like swords. He would run to meet them. He ran, stopping only to pull a branch of thorns from under his foot" (204).

As Deven sees it, his alliance with Nur requires a responsibility that cannot be abjured, even after the poet's death:

> Where was the end? Was there one? He had a vision of Nur's bier, white, heaped with flowers. He saw the women in the family weeping and wailing around it. He saw the shroud, the grave open. When Nur was laid in it, would this connection break, this relation end? No, never—the bills would come to him, he would have to pay for the funeral, support the widows, raise his son. He had accepted the gift of Nur's poetry and that meant he was custodian of Nur's very soul and spirit. It was a great distinction. He could not deny or abandon that under any pressure. (204)

In other words, it dawns on the narrator that the call of the present cannot be ignored in favor of a regression into an edenic past that distorts current realities. Such a regression would cause the individual to be devoured by the forces of rapacious change symbolized by the transformation of Nur's pigeons from being "a symbol of flight and charm": "a flock of pigeons had swooped down out of the coppery sky and blocked his (poet's) way with their hurtling wings and violently struggling bodies" (47). This mythic realm does not have the potential to reinterpret repressive frameworks in order to deploy "the balanced and reasonable approach of critical realism that encourages one to retain faith in human complexity as opposed to the static stereotyping that results from fixation on ignoble aspects of myth" (Afzal-Khan 90). But hearkening to the call of the present should not necessitate a rejection of a rich cultural heritage and traditions—as Nur's poetry and Urdu literature as well as Muslim culture are in danger of being incorporated and neutralized within a nationalist polity that annihilates the nuances woven by cultural and linguistic differences in post-Independence India.

Having donned the mantle of the custodian of the poet's work, Deven's final acceptance of life with fortitude is indicative of the emergence of a "self" that has relinquished the safety of illusory myths and yet has arrived at a rapturous affirmation of existence, as we can see from the following passage, in which the narrator is lost in contemplation after Nur's funeral:

> The sky was filling with a gray light that was dissolving the dense darkness of night. It glistened upon a field of white pampas grass which waved in a sudden breeze that had sprung up, laughing waving and rustling through the grass with a live, rippling sound. (204)

His acceptance of responsibility for Nur's work entails accepting responsibility of Nur's wives and all they signify. Through Deven's ability to accept the petty, sordid, and disgusting realities as part of art, rather than its demonized outside, Desai challenges the decapacitation of an existence that is created by traditions that do not stand the test of realities thrown in their way by history. The author depicts the cultural and social transformations that India has undergone in its postcolonial phase. Desai's deconstruction of the domestic and cultural worlds created by gender norms and gender roles in *In Custody* is, in effect, an ironic comment on the centralizing nationalist ideals emphasized by the nation's rhetoric even today.

As Judie Newman points out, Desai analyzes the relationship of literature to history and concludes that history, for Desai, is not "a silenced story, but neither can it be rewritten at random" (45). Desai says that the dominant theme of her works is "the terror of facing single-handed, the ferocious assaults of existence" (Libert 47). Desai's works have won critical and literary acclaim in India and in the West. Critics commend the profoundly psychological depth of her fiction that brings her existentialist view of life into relief.

Desai received the National Academy of Letters Award for *Fire on the Mountain* (1977), and the Guardian Prize for Children's fiction for *The Village by the Sea* (1982). Her *Clear Light of Day* (1980), and *In Custody* (1984), were nominated for the Booker Award of the United Kingdom. Desai started her writing career with a short story in an American children's magazine. Since then she has published twelve books of fiction and many essays, reviews, and articles. *Games at Twilight* (1978), is a collection of short stories, the rest of her books are novels.

Critical responses to *In Custody* focus largely on the portrayal of Deven as a character with "human value and interest," which "with such a dreary, feeble spirit as Deven is evidence of a rare gift for creating something completely authentic and true" (Walsh 112). According to Sebastian Faulks, the novel is a "prolonged comedy of exasperation" that "strains toward allegory" because Deven appears to be a "mere embodiment of goodness" (26). But I have argued that Desai's portrayal of the characters in her novel, *In Custody,* renders it a complex work that demystifies the concept of the nation as a space in which various forms of identification can be filled: racial, religious, linguistic, cultural, historical, and geographical. She attempts to excise the sterile and dysfunctional aspects of a culture in order to dispel nostalgic nationalist myths and ushers in a transnational era in which a nation is not constructed around a common language, religion, culture, patriarchal image of womanhood, and an ethnically pure majority, which will eliminate minorities.

Conclusion

> Translation becomes central to the migrant's experience in the metro-
> politan or postcolonial city, as she or he takes on the more active role of
> cultural translator. Having translated themselves, migrants then
> encounter there other translated men and women, other restless mar-
> ginals, and translate their experiences to each other to form new lan-
> guages of desire and affirmation: circuits of activism, circuits of desire.
> (Young 142)

In this study, I have attempted to appreciate the various social and historical
contexts of writing, reading, and language in order to empower me to negotiate the space between the two cultural realities that I straddle—Kashmiri and
American. What is it to be a western-educated Kashmiri Muslim woman in the
U.S.? This has been a difficult struggle. On the one hand, I have assiduously
attempted to refuse creating a disharmonious relationship between my culture,
religion, social mores, and myself; on the other hand, I have tried to steer clear
of the ever-present temptation to dwell in a mythical past.

Kashmir, an idyllic haven in the foothills of the Himalayas, is a space in
which conflicting discourses have been written and read. Cultural notions of
Kashmiris in image and word have been reconstructed to emphasize the bias
that reinforces the propagandist agenda of the hegemonic powers involved in
the Kashmir dispute, India and Pakistan. In establishment Indian and Pakistani
thought, Kashmiris are defined as different from the nationals of the two countries. The various fractions in the state of Jammu & Kashmir, Kashmiri Muslims, Kashmiri Pandits, Dogras, and Ladakhis, have tried time and again to
form a national consciousness in order to name its cultural alterity through the
nation, as "Kashmiriyat." But due to the regional sentiments that are so well
entrenched in the psyche of the people, this attempt is still in a volatile stage.
The symbols of nationhood in Jammu & Kashmir, flag, anthem, and constitution, have thus far been unable to forge the process of nationalist self-imagining.
Although, separatist movements have been surfacing and resurfacing since the

accession of Kashmir to India in 1947, the attempt to create a unitary cultural identity bolstered by nationalist politics has been subverted by regional political forces and the comprador class, backed-up by the governments of India and Pakistan. The revolutionary acts of demanding the right of self-determination and autonomy for Jammu & Kashmir have not been able to nurture a unity amongst all socioeconomic classes.

Kashmiris have tried, time and again, to translate themselves from passive recipients of violence legitimated by the foreign legislations of the physically and psychologically removed parliaments of India and Pakistan into subjects who recognize that they can exercise agency and take control of their destinies.[1] They march forward with a refusal to allow history to be imposed on them; now the people of Kashmir attempt to take charge of their social and political destinies. The insistence on rejecting the trajectory charted out for them by the power structures of India, Pakistan, and the West and the urge to proclaim themselves a nation that is capable of exercising the right of self-determination has been haunting the psyche of the Kashmiri people for decades. Over the years, tremendous political and social turmoil has been generated in the state by the forces of religious fundamentalism and by an exclusionary nationalism that seeks to erode the cultural syncretism that is part of the ethos of Kashmir. These forces are responsible for the shutting down of dissenters who voice cultural critique, repression of women, political anarchy, economic deprivation, lack of infrastructure, and mass displacements that have been occasioned by these events.

In book I put forth my cultural knowledge as an oppositional discursive system to imperialist ideologies that purport to create a "civilizing mission," creating a totalizing or homogenizing center, thereby generating a dialectical interplay. I recognize the centrality of non-Western cultural, religious, political, and social epistemologies that have been dismissed as "marginal" or reductively "fanatical" by the dominant discourse. Some of these epistemologies are the constructs, institutions, and modes of thought created by contemporary cultural nationalisms; the consciousness of political, social, and cultural place that offers a critical perspective from which to formulate alternatives to an insulated modernity and its concomitant political defeatism of Third-World nations; the demystification of the concept of the nation and the ushering in of an era in which a nation is not constructed around a common language, religion, culture, patriarchal image of womanhood, and an ethnically pure majority.

The drama of my book lies in the intricate politics created by the intertwined phenomena of nationalism, transnationalism, and fundamentalism in the postcolonial realm. On the one hand, the nation is perceived as a receptacle in which racial, religious, linguistic, cultural, historical, and geographical identification can be filled. On the other hand, transnational cultural, political, and economic practices and identities can lead to the politicization of identity in the form of fundamentalism, xenophobia, and a fanatical espousal of tradition inflected by gender.[2]

Women in postcolonial countries are positioned in relation to their own cultural realities, their own histories, their sensitivity to the diversity of cultural traditions and to the questions and conflicts within them, their own struggles not just with the legacies of colonialism but also with the centralizing hegemony of the cultural nationalism propagated in the postcolony, their own relations to the West, their interpretations of religious law, and their concepts of the role of women in contemporary societies.[3]

Nationalist movements and literatures of independence have portrayed women as icons of cultural preservation. In the postcolonial phase of nations, gender divisions have been reinforced by the hallowed figure of the "third-world woman" (Gandhi 83). I oppose this decapacitating iconicity of "woman" that traditional Islamic, Hindu, and Victorian concepts of femininity endorse. The rich complexity in the social and cultural positions of "third-world women" is ignored in order to retain the remnants of colonialist power-knowledge in "[the] appropriation and codification of 'scholarship' and 'knowledge' about women in the third world by particular analytic categories . . ." (Mohanty 196). But this complexity is also ignored to preserve the nationalist portraits of the "native woman," which do not concede to the female subject the right to foreground her own "distinct actualities" (Minh-ha 5).

I seek to reinterpret the repressive frameworks of colonialism, nationalism, proto-nationalism, patriarchy, and universalism that essentialize the identities of postcolonial and transnational subjects. The linguistic and cultural dislocation generated by the experience of migration can become part of the process of achieving control because as the displaced group is assimilated its native language and culture become devalued. The schism created by this dislocation is bridged when formerly repressed voices from the non-European world are raised in order to foreground the cultural and historical perspectives external to Europe. One of the ways of including this perspective is to encourage a rewriting of history that incorporates profound religious, cultural, and linguistic differences into the text, and narrates the history of the nationalist struggle in a form which negates colonial historiography (Rushdie 1981, 1988; Ghosh 1988). This kind of radical politics of postcolonialism seeks to bridge the schism created by the vast difference between the experience of place and the cultural perspective and language available to it. I have argued that in the space of transnationalism, cultures undergo a dialectical interplay and create interlayered and mixed identities. This process necessitates the reconception and incorporation of cultural and linguistic differences into our sense of identity. My transnational identity gives me a means of questioning elements not just of my native culture but of Western culture as well. As Edward W. Said articulates,

> The exile knows that in a secular and contingent world, homes are always provisional. Borders and barriers which enclose us within the safety of familiar territory can also become prisons, and are often defended beyond reason or necessity. Exiles cross borders, break barriers of thought and experience. (365)

The recognition that all historical and social events can be understood within more than one explanatory framework has given me the critical tools with which to expound on the variability of spaces that I, as a transnational subject occupy. The diverse possibilities of interpretation that are generated in these spaces, cultural nationalism, religious fundamentalism, patriarchal dominance, and cultural hybridity, have given me the enriching opportunity to imagine new possibilities for myself.[4]

Appendix

Although postcolonial criticisms, theories, and literatures, to borrow the words of Bill Ashcroft et al., scrutinize the methodology by "which Europe imposed and maintained its codes in its colonial domination of so much of the rest of the world" (*Empire* 196), I wonder to what extent postcolonial writers are successful in foregrounding national and regional perspectives in their texts. Does postcolonial discourse overlook demarcations between various socioeconomic classes, religions, histories, sexual orientations, and politics? Is it oblivious to the perniciousness of the universal "truths" perpetuated by the single domain within which ideological and political practices are articulated?

South Asian historiography, according to the *Subaltern Studies* team, puts the postcolonial subject either in the category of the barbaric, ignorant, "other" against which civilized Europe defines itself or in the category of pure, authentic, unquestionable icon of the nation. Too often, postcoloniality is limited to merely a transnational condition. In other words, it relegates the social and economic particulars of the postcolony into the background. By doing so, postcoloniality creates for immigrants a liminal zone that obscures the fact that not all of them have the same access to the transnational space created by the economic and cultural movement of labor and capital in the post-imperialist era. For example, South Asian in the U.K. and in the Caribbean immigrated to these regions as indentured labor, and had to perform menial tasks in order to make ends meet. Even today, a lot of these immigrants are on the lowest rung of the social and economic ladder. One example of the incorporation of South Asian immigrants into the British infrastructure would be the palpable hierarchy at one of the busiest international airports in the world, Heathrow in London. Heathrow is evocative of a filthy railway station in India, where all the janitors, cleaning ladies, and sales people at kiosks are Indian. The air crackles with the sonorous sounds of Punjabi, and the smell of Indian food wafts toward the jet-lagged passenger making a peaceful nap, a pipedream. On the contrary, South Asian immigrants in the U.S. are a part of the group that caused a brain-drain in the country of origin when it shifted its geographical location. Jane Singh et al. provide some interesting statistics regarding the physical movement of South Asian labor and capital to the U.S., "In numerical terms, South Asian did not register a significant demographic presence in Anglo-America till the 1960s, when the Canadian government removed racial and national immigration restrictions . . . And President Lyndon B. Johnson signed the Act of 3 October 1965 . . . , which eliminated race, religion, and nationality as criteria for immigration and phased out the quota system in the United States" (18). The scrimpy presence of South Asians in the U.S. prior to that era was transformed by the creation of new vistas of communication between the peoples of the globe. These vistas of exchange and communication were the spaces in which various modes of representation and cultural praxes grappled with and influenced one another. I have tried to answer the following questions in this work: Does transnationalism enable an equal exchange between metropolitan modes of representation and those of the "Third-World"? How have metropolitan constructions of subordinated others been shaped by those others?

Notes

NOTES TO CHAPTER ONE

1. The experiences of cultural transition forced by the colonial encounter cause the dislocation of formerly colonized subjects. A dislocated self is inevitable for the transmigrant subject, especially in the South Asian context, where the vigor of a literate culture resisted the deracination that pervaded creolized societies.

2. This multifaceted vision creates comminglings in the language of narration of transnational texts. The commingling of genres helps the migrant writer to defuse the elements of "otherness" that are created by marginalized voices. This mediation of genres is a "strategy of liberation" (Afzal-Khan 154), similar to the necessity for cultural improvisations, whether at "home" or "abroad," stressed by Ghosh, the author in exile from the cultural forms of his South Asian past.

NOTES TO CHAPTER TWO

1. The form of Islam as practiced in these nations does not enable the creation of a hybridized consciousness like Rushdie's, Ghosh's, and Desai's.

2. These divisions reveal the constructed and manipulated nature of nation" and "nationalism" (Anderson 1983; Bhabha 1990; Boehmer 1991; Brennan 1989; Chatterjee 1993; Hobsbawm 1990).

3. Mohun Biswas fails to perceive identity as a dialectical historical reality.

NOTES TO CHAPTER THREE

1. Brennan concludes that, "Their shockingly inappropriate juxtaposition of humorous matter-of-factness and appallingly accurate violence, both ironically alludes to the blasé reporting of contemporary news and the preventable horrors of current events" (34).

2. The metaphor of "chutnification" suggests myth and magic through its "magical"—and foreign to Western culinary traditions—blend of sweet, sour, and spicy tastes.

3. Jaina C. Sanga analyzes the kipper in this incident as "an emblematic metonym for the new homeland. . . . The kipper is also something through which Saladin can assert and ascribe a sense of English identity, represented as victory" (35).

4. Like one of the characters in *Midnight's Children,* Aadam Aziz, and the protagonist in *Shame,* Omar Khayyam, Saladin perceives "home" as an oppressive reality that he longs to escape.

5. Again, as with the sense of displacement that tortures Aadam Aziz and Saleem in *Midnight's Children,* and the plight of the characters in *Shame* who have migrated to the new nation-state of Pakistan from their original homeland, Saladin is torn apart by his longings for purity and permanence in the face of the impurity and intermingling all around him.

NOTES TO CHAPTER FOUR

1. Tridib is the curious eight-year-old narrator's mentor and narrates these historically significant events to the child.

2. As Suvir Kaul notes, each time communal violence rears its ugly head, the horrific memories of Partition resurface (*Partitions* 3).

3. For example, each time the story of the Partition is related in the Indian context in order to demonstrate the reprehensibility of the Muslim League and negate the damaging role played by religious zealots within the Indian National Congress, the "official" account of the partition worsens religious and social divisions (Kaul, *Partitions* 7).

4. Humanism refers to a view of the world that exalts a human freedom and agency not limited by the linguistic, political, cultural, and socioeconomic conditions of existence.

5. Commenting on her role in the novel, Kaul notes that Ila functions as "a narrative scapegoat, a figure who acts as a lightning-rod for a great many sexual and cultural anxieties, and the telling of whose unhappy and even sordid itinerary takes on all the cautionary tones of a modern fable" ("Separation Anxiety" 130).

6. Her nationalist ideology, according to Rahul Sapra is "one which 'shuts other people out'; which defines 'Us' against 'Them'" (59).

7. Robert J. C. Young informs us that, "According to an extensively documented report published in 2002, the explosive growth of Hindutva in India, which has under-girded much of the sectarian communal violence of the last decades, has been amply funded by a U.S. charity, the India Development and Relief Fund, based in Maryland, despite U.S. laws prohibiting such charities from engaging in political activities. Money from non-resident Indians in the U.S. creates the link between the idealized past and its

violent production by state governments and non-governmental organizations in the present" (63).

NOTES TO CHAPTER FIVE

1. Chandra Talpade Mohanty observes that the employment of "women" as a category assumes an "ahistorical, universal unity between women based on a generalized notion of their subordination" (64).

2. Chandra Chatterjee tells us about the traumatic vicissitudes to which the women of the two newly carved out nation-states were subjected, "official figures estimate that 33,000 non-Muslim women in Pakistan and 50,000 Muslim women in India were separated from their families either because they were lost during the dispersal and abandoned, or else because they were abducted as an act of community revenge inspired by hatred" (102).

3. In another instance, the crime of a boy from a lower social caste against a woman from a higher upper caste in the Meerawala village in the central province of Punjab in Pakistan was punished in a revealing way by the "sagacious" tribal jury. After days of thoughtful consideration, this jury gave the verdict that the culprit's teenage sister, Mai, should be gang-raped by a group of goons from the wronged social group: "Village councils are often convened in rural areas to settle local disputes and women often end up as pawns of village elders. Mai said she went to the council after her young brother Abdul Shakoor was kidnapped by a rival family and accused of raping one of its members. Mai's Gujar family said Shakoor was sodomized by Mastoi men as a punishment. The council ruled that to save the honor of the Mastoi clan, Shakoor should marry the woman with whom he was linked while Mai was to be given away in marriage to a Mastoi man. The prosecution said that when she rejected the decision she was gang-raped by four Mastoi men and made to walk home semi-naked in front of hundreds of people. The lawyer for one of the accused argued the rape charge was invalid because Mai was technically married to the defendant at the time of the incident" (Reuters).

NOTES TO THE CONCLUSION

1. I agree with Jonathan Culler's distinction between agency subject positions: "There is much to be gained . . . From separating the concepts of subject position and of agency, recognizing that they belong to different sorts of narratives" (121).

2. "Despite some countertendencies towards pluralism and multi-faith protestations, world religions often seem to develop a proclivity towards ecumenism, orthodoxy or fundamentalism" (Cohen 188). I might add that the political philosophy of world religions like Islam, Hinduism, Christianity, Judaism, and Buddhism is guided by transterritorial rather than territorial aims.

3. "For this reason, postcolonial politics has often more in common with women's than men's struggles of the colonial era, with a politics of diversity rather than the cultural uniformity demanded for nationalism" (Young 99).

4. As Judith Butler explains, "the reconceptualization of identity as an effect, that is, as produced or generated opens up possibilities of 'agency' that are insidiously foreclosed by positions that take identity categories as foundational and fixed" (147). Butler locates agency in possibilities created in the variability of spaces that create identity.

Bibliography

Afzal-Khan, Fawzia. *Cultural Imperialism and the Indo-English Novel: Genre and Ideology in R. K. Narayan, Anita Desai, Kamala Markandaya, and Salman Rushdie.* Philadelphia: U of Pennsylvania P, 1993.

Ahmad, Aijaz. *In Theory: Classes, Nations, Literatures.* London: Verso, 1992.

———. *Lineages of the Present: Ideology and Politics in Contemporary South Asia.* New York: Verso, 2000.

Anderson, Benedict. *Imagined Communities: Reflections on the Origin and Spread of Nationalism.* London: Verso, 1983.

Appadurai, Arjun. *Modernity at Large: Cultural Dimensions of Globalization.* Minneapolis: U of Minnesota P, 1996.

Appignanesi, Lisa and Sara Maitland, eds. *The Rushdie File.* London: Fourth Estate, 1989.

Ashcroft, Bill, Gareth Griffins, and Helen Tiffin, eds. *The Empire Writes Back.* New York: Routledge, 1989.

———. *Key Concepts in Post-Colonial Theory.* New York: Routledge, 1989.

Baudrillard, Jean. *The Transparency of Evil: Essays on Extreme Phenomena.* New York: Verso, 1993.

Bhabha, Homi. *The Location of Culture.* London: Routledge, 1994.

———. *Nation and Narration.* New York: Routledge, 1990.

Boehmer, Elleke. *Colonial and Postcolonial Literature.* Oxford: Oxford UP, 1995.

———. *Empire, the National, and the Postcolonial, 1890–1920: Resistance in Interaction.* New York: Oxford UP, 2002.

Brass, Paul R. "Elite Competition and Nation-Formation." *Nationalism.* Ed. John Hutchinson and Anthony D. Smith. Oxford: Oxford UP, 1994.

Brecht, Bertolt. *The Rise and Fall of the City of Mahagonny. Collected Plays of Bertolt Brecht.* Ed. John Willett and Ralph Manhein. London: Metheun, 1985.

Brennan, Timothy. *Salman Rushdie and the Third World: Myths of the Nation.* London: Macmillan, 1989.

Butler, Judith. *Bodies that Matter: On the Discursive Limits of "Sex."* New York: Routledge, 1993.

Cary, Joyce. *Aissa Saved.* London: Michael Joseph, 1949.

Chakrabarty, U. "Whatever Happened to the Vedic Dasi? Orientalism, Nationalism, and a Script for the Past." *Recasting Women: Essays in Colonial History.* Ed. Kum Kum Sangari and Sudesh Vaid. Delhi: Kali for Women, 1989.

Chatterjee, Chandra. *Surviving Colonialism: A Study of R. K. Narayan, Anita Desai, V. S. Naipaul.* New Delhi: Radha Publications, 2000.

Chatterjee, Partha. *The Nation and its Fragments: Colonial and Postcolonial Histories.* Princeton: Princeton UP, 1993.

Cohen, Robin. *Global Diasporas: An Introduction.* London: UCL Press, 1997.

Cole, John. *The International Flow of Information: A Trans-Pacific Perspective.* Washington D. C.: Library of Congress, 1981.

Conner, Walker. "The Impact of Homelands Upon Diasporas." *Modern Diasporas in International Politics.* Ed. Gabriel Sheffer. New York: St. Martin's P, 1986. 16–46.

Conrad, Joseph. *Heart of Darkness.* Ed. Paul O'Prey. Harmondsworth: Penguin, 1983.

Cuoto, Mary. Review of *The Shadow Lines. Times Literary Supplement* 4465 28 Oct. 1988: 1212.

Culler, Jonathan. *Literary Theory: A Very Short Introduction.* Oxford: Oxford UP, 1997.

Davis, Horace B. *Towards a Marxist Theory of Nationalism.* New York: Monthly Review P, 1978.

Desai, Anita. *Clear Light of Day.* London: Penguin, 1980.

——. *Fire on the Mountain.* London: Heinemann, 1977.

——. *Games at Twilight: And Other Stories.* Hardmondsworth: Penguin, 1978.

——. *In Custody.* New York: Harper and Row, 1984.

——. "Replies to the Questionnaire." *Kakatiya Journal of English Studies* 3.1 (1978): 1–6.

——. *The Village by the Sea.* London: Heinemann, 1982.

Descartes, René. *Discourse on Method and Meditations.* New York: Liberal Arts P, 1960.

Dhondy, Farukh. "Indian Writers Don't Know Why Their Country Is In Such a Mess." *Literary Review* Aug. 13, 2001: 1–7.

Erickson, John. *Islam and Postcolonial Narrative.* Cambridge: Cambridge UP, 1998.

Faiz, Faiz Ahmad. "The Dawn of Freedom, August 1947." *The Rebel's Silhouette: Selected Poems: Poetry of Faiz Ahmad Faiz.* Trans. Agha Shahid Ali. Salt Lake City: Peregrine Smith Books, 1991. 16–21.

Fanon, Frantz. *Wretched of the Earth.* Trans. Constance Farrington. Harmondsworth: Penguin, 1986.

Faulks, Sebastian. "Straining Towards Allegory." Review of *In Custody. Books and Bookmen* 350 (Nov. 1984): 26.

Forster, E. M. *A Passage to India.* London: Dent, 1942.

Françoise, Pierre. "Salman Rushdie's Philosophical Materialism in *The Satanic Verses.*" *Reading Rushdie: Perspectives on the Fiction of Salman Rushdie.* Ed. M. D. Fletcher. Amsterdam: Rodopi, 1984. 305–20.

Friese, Kai. "Hijacking India's History." *New York Times* Dec. 30, 2002: sec. A: 17.

Gandhi, Leela. *Postcolonial Theory: A Critical Introduction.* New York: Columbia UP, 1998.

Ghosh, Amitav. *The Calcutta Chromosome.* New York: Avon Books, 1995.

———. *The Circle of Reason.* New York: Viking Penguin, 1986.

———. "The Diaspora in Indian Culture." *Public Culture* 2.1 (1989): 75–7.

———. *The Glass Palace.* New York: Random House, 2001.

———. *In an Antique Land.* New York: Knopf, 1993.

———. *The Shadow Lines.* New York: Viking, 1989.

———. "Shadow Script." Interview. *First City.* New Delhi. Sep. 2000.

Gill, Raj. *The Rape.* New Delhi: Sterling Publishers, 1974.

Glick Schiller, Nina, Linda Basch, and Caol Blanc-Szanton. "Transnationalism: A New Analtyical Framework for Understanding Migration." *Towards a Transnational Perspective on Migration: Race, Class, Ethnicity and Nationalism Reconsidered.* Ed. Nina Glick Schiller, Linda Basch, and Caol Blanc-Szanton. New York: New York Academy of Sciences, 1992. 1–24.

Godard, Jean Luc. *Alphaville: A Film.* Rev. ed. London: Lorrimer, 1984.

Goodheart, Eugene. "V. S. Naipaul's Mandarin Sensibility." *Partisan Review* 50 (1983): 244–56.

Grant, Damien. *Salman Rushdie.* London: Northcote House Publishers, 1999.

Guarnizo, Luis Eduardo and Michael Peter Smith. "The Locations of Trannationalism." *Transnationalism From Below.* Ed. Michael Peter Smith and Luis Eduardo Guarnizo. New Brunswick: Transaction Publishers, 1998. 3–34.

Guha, Ranajit. "On Some Aspects of the Historiography of Colonial India." *Subaltern Studies I: Writings on South Asian History and Society.* Ed. Ranajit Guha. New Delhi: Oxford UP, 1982. 1–8.

Guptara, Prabhu S. *Black British Literature: An Annotated Bibliography.* Mundelstrup: Dangaroo Press, 1986.

Hamilton, Ian. "The First Life of Salman Rushdie." *New Yorker* 25 Dec. 1995: 90–7, 110–113, 112–13.

Hassunami, Sabrina. *Salman Rushdie: A Postmodern Reading of His Major Works.* Madison: Fairleigh Dickinson UP, 2002.

Hobsbawm, Eric J. *Nations and Nationalism Since 1780.* Cambridge: Cambridge UP, 1990.

Hower, Edward. Review of *The Shadow Lines. New York Times Book Review* 2 July 1989: 10.

India. Census Commissioner. *Census of India, 1951.* Delhi: Manager of Publications, 1952-.

Indira, S. *Anita Desai as an Artist: A Study in Image and Symbol.* New Delhi: Creative Books, 1994.

Jacobson, Matthew F. *Special Sorrows: The Diaporic Imagination of Irish, Polish, and Jewish Immigrants in the United States.* Cambridge: Harvard UP, 1995.

Jain, Jasbir. *Stairs to the Attic: The Novels of Anita Desai.* Jaipur: Printwell Publishers, 1987.

Jameson, Fredric. "Postmodernism and Consumer Society." *The Anti-Aesthetic: Essays on Postmodern Culture.* Ed. Hal Foster. Port Townsend: Bay P, 1983.

JanMohamad, Abdul R. "The Economy of Manichean Allegory: The Function Of Racial Difference in Colonialist Literature." *Critical Inquiry* 12.1 (1985): 59–87.

Johnson, Patrick. "V. S. Naipaul." *Black Scholar* 15.3 (1984): 12–14.

Karamcheti, Indira. "The Geographics of Marginality: Place and Textuality in Simone Schwarz-Bart and Anita Desai." *Reconfigured Spaces: Feminist Explorations of Literary Space.* Ed. Margaret R. Higonnet and Joan Templeton. Amherst: U of Massachusetts P, 1994. 125–46.

Kaul, A. N. "A Reading of *The Shadow Lines.*" *The Shadow Lines.* By Amitav Ghosh. Delhi: Oxford UP, 1995. 299–309.

Kaul, Suvir. Introduction. *The Partitions of Memory: Afterlife of the Division of India.* Ed. Suvir Kaul. Indiana: Indiana UP, 2001. 1-29.

——. "Separation Anxiety: Growing Up Inter/National in Amitav Ghosh's *The Shadow Lines.*" *The Oxford Literary Review* 16 (1994): 125–45.

Kaura, Uma. *Muslims and Indian Nationalism: The Emergence of the Demand for India's Partition 1928–40.* Columbia: South Asia Books, 1977.

Kipling, Rudyard. *Kim.* London: Macmillan, 1963.

Krishnaswamy, Revathi. "Mythologies of Migrancy." *Ariel: A Review of International World Literature.* 26.1 (1995): 125–46.

Kumar, Amitava. *Bombay-London-New York.* New York: Routledge, 2002.

Lewis, Bernard. *Islam and the West.* New York: Oxford UP, 1993.

Libert, Florence. "An Interview with Anita Desai, 1 August 1989. Cambridge. England." *World Literature Written in English* 30:1 (1990): 47–55.

Malgonkar, Manohar. *A Bend in the Ganges: A Novel.* New York: Viking Press, 1965.

Mariana, Phil. *The Politics of Imaginative Writing.* Seattle: Bay Press, 1991.

Martin, Murray S. "Order, Disorder, and Rage in the Islands: The Novels of V. S. Naipaul and Albert Wendt." *Perspectives on Contemporary Literature* 10 (1984): 33–39.l.

Marzorati, Gerald. "Fiction's Embattled Infidel." *New York Times* 26 Jan. 1989: 33–56.

Mayaram, Shail. "Speech, Silence and the Making of Partition Violence in Mewar." *Subaltern Studies IX: Writings on South Asian History and Society.* Ed. Shahid Amin and Dipesh Chakrabarty. New Delhi: Oxford UP, 1996. 126–63.

McClintock, Ann. *Dangerous Liaisons: Gender, Nation, and Postcolonial Perspective.* Minneapolis: U of Minnesota P, 1997.

Mee, Jon. "After Midnight: The Novel in the 1980s and 1990s." *A History of Indian Literature in English.* Ed. Arvind Krishna Mehrotra. New York: Columbia, 2003. 318–36.

Minh-ha, Trinh T. *Woman, Native, Other.* Bloomington: Indiana UP, 1989.

Mishra, Vijay. "Diasporas and the Art of Impossible Meaning." *In Diaspora: Theories, Histories, Texts.* Ed. Makarand Paranjape. New Delhi: Indialog Publications, 2001.

Mohanty, Chandra. "Under Western Eyes: Feminist Scholarship and Colonial Discourses." *Third World Women and the Politics of Feminism.* Bloomington: Indiana UP, 1991. 50–65.

Mohanty, Chandra Talpade, Ann Russo, and Lourdes Torres. *Third World Women and the Politics of Feminism.* Bloomington: Indiana UP, 1991.

Mohanty, Satya. *Literary Theory and the Claims of History: Postmodernism, Objectivity, Multicultural Politics.* Ithaca: Cornell UP, 1997.

Mortimer, Edward. *People, Nation and State: The Meaning of Ethnicity and Nationalism.* New York: I.B. Tauris, 1999.

Mukherjee, Arun. *Towards an Aesthetic of Opposition: Essays on Criticism and Cultural Imperialism.* Stratford: Williams-Wallace, 1988.

Mukherjee, Meenakshi. "Maps and Mirrors: Co-ordinates of Meaning in *The Shadow Lines.*" *The Shadow Lines.* By Amitav Ghosh. Delhi: Oxford UP, 1995. 255–67.

Naipaul, V. S. *Among the Believers: An Islamic Journey.* London: Deutsch, 1981.

——. *Beyond Belief: Islamic Excursions Among the Converted People.* London: Little, Brown, 1998.

——. *A House for Mr. Biswas.* London: Deutsch, 1961.

——. *India: A Wounded Civilization.* London: Deutsch, 1977.

——. *The Middle Passage; Impressions of Five Societies: British, French, and Dutch in the West Indies and South America.* New York: Macmillan, 1963.

——. *The Mimic Men.* London: Deutsch, 1967.

——. *The Mystic Masseur.* Hardsworth: Penguin Books, 1957.

——. *The Suffrage of Elvira.* London: Deutsch, 1958.

——. qtd. in "Writer Without Roots." Mell Gussow. *The New York Times Magazine* 26 December 1976: 19–22,

Nairn, Tom. *The Break-up of Britain: Crisis and Neo-Nationalism.* London: New Left Books, 1977.

Nandy, Ashish. *The Intimate Enemy: Loss and Recovery of Self Under Colonialism.* Oxford: Oxford UP, 1983.

Narayan, Shyamala A. and Jon Mee. "Novelists of the 1950s and 1960s." *A History of Indian Literature in English.* Ed. Arvind Krishns Mehrotra. New York: Columbia, 2003. 219–31.

Needham, Anuradha Dingwaney. "The Politics of Post-Colonial Identity in Salman Rushdie." *Reading Rushdie: Perspectives on the Fiction of Salman Rushdie.* Ed. M. D. Fletcher. Amsterdam: Rodopi, 1994. 149–57.

Nelson, Emmanuel S. *Reworlding: The Literature of the Indian Diaspora.* New York: Greenwood P, 1992.

Newman, Judie. "History and Letters: Anita Desai's Baumgartner's Bombay." *World Literature Written in English* 30:1 (1990): 37–46.

Pakistan. Office of the Census Commissioner. *Census of Pakistan, 1951, Village List.* Karachi: Manager of Publications, 1952.

Parnell, Tim. "Salman Rushdie: From Colonial Politics to Postmodern Politics." *Writing India 1757–1900: The Literature of British India.* Ed. Bart Moore-Gilbert. Manchester: Manchester UP, 1996. 254–7.

Pipes, Daniel. *The Rushdie Affair: The Novel, the Ayatollah, and the West.* New York: Birch Lane, 1990.

Prakash, Gyan, ed. *After Colonialism: Imperial Histories and Post-Colonial Displacements.* Princeton: Princeton UP, 1995.

Prasad, Murari. "The Shadow Lines: A Quest for Invisible Sanity." *The Novels of Amitav Ghosh.* Ed. R. K. Dhawan. New Delhi: Prestige Books, 1991. 87–95.

Rachlin, Nahid. *The Foreigner.* New York: Norton, 1978.

Rajan, Balachandra. *The Dark Dancer: a Novel.* Westport: Greenwood Press, 1970.

Rao, Bhaskar U. *The Story of Rehabilitation.* Delhi: Department of Rehabilitation, Ministry of Labor, Employment & Rehabilitation, Government of India, 1967.

Reuters. "Pakistan Court Expected to Rule on Gang-Rape Case." *Khaleej Times* 27 August 2002. 22 August 2003 http://www.khaleejtimes.co.ae/ktarchive/270802/subcont.htm.

Roy, Arundhati. "Fascism's Firm Footprint in India." *Nation* September 30 2002: 16–20.

Rushdie, Salman. *Grimus.* London: Grafton, 1975.

——. *Haroun and the Sea of Stories.* New York: Granta, 1990.

——. "Imaginary Homelands." *Imaginary Homelands: Essays and Criticism, 1981–1991.* London: Granta, 1991.

——. *Imaginary Homelands: Essays and Criticism, 1981–1991.* London: Granta, 1991.

——. "In Good Faith." *Imaginary Homelands: Essays and Criticism, 1981–1991.* New York: Granta, 1991.

——. "The Indian Writer in England." *The Eye of the Beholder: Indian Writing in English.* Ed. Maggie Butcher. London: Commonwealth Institute, 1983.

——. *Midnight's Children.* London: Cape, 1981.

——. *The Moor's Last Sigh.* London: Cape, 1995.

——. "Pen Against the Sword: In Good Faith." *Newsweek* 12 February 1990: 52–7.

——. *The Satanic Verses.* London: Viking, 1988.

——. *Shame.* London: Cape, 1983.

Ruthven, Malise. *A Satanic Affair: Salman Rushdie and the Wrath of Islam.* London: Chatto, 1991.

Sahgal, Nayantara. "The Schizophrenic Imagination." *From Commonwealth to Post-Colonial.* Ed. Anna Rutherford. Mundelstrup: Dangaroo Press, 1992.

Said, Edward W. *Culture and Imperialism.* New York: Knopf: Distributed by Random House, 1993.

——. *Orientalism.* New York: Vintage Books, 1979.

——. "Reflections on Exile." *Out There: Marginalization and Contemporary Cultures.* Ed. R. Ferguson et. Al. Cambridge: MIT Press, 1990. 357–63.

Sanga, Jaina. *Salman Rushdie's Postcolonial Metaphors: Migration, Translation, Hybridity, Blasphemy, and Globalization.* Westport: Greenwood Press, 2001.

Sapra, Rahul. "The Shadow Lines and the Questioning of Nationalism." *The Fiction of Amitav Ghosh.* Ed. Indira Bhatt and Indira Nityanandam. New Delhi: Creative Books, 2001. 57–65.

Satchidanandan, K. "That Third Space: Interrogating the Diasporic Paradigm." *In Diaspora: Theories, Histories, Texts.* Ed. Makarand Paranjape. New Delhi: Indialog Publications, 2001. 15–23.

Shabestari, Mohammad Mojtahed. *A Critique of the Official Reading of eligion.* Tehran: Tarh e Publications, 2000.

Sheffer, Gabriel. *Diaspora Politics.* Cambridge: Cambridge UP, 2003.

Sidhwa, Bapsi. *Ice-Candy-Man.* London: William Heinemann, 1988.

Simmel, George. "The Number of Members as Determining the Sociological Form of the Group." *The American Journal of Sociology* 8.1 (1902): 1–46.

Singh, Jane, Emily Hodges, Bruce La Brack, and Kenneth R. Logan. *South Asians in North America: an Annotated & Selected Bibliography.* Berkeley: Center for South and Southeast Asia Studies, University of California, Berkeley, 1988.

Singh, Khushwant. *A Train to Pakistan.* New York: Grove Press, 1956.

Slemon, Stephen. *Magic Realism: Theory, History, Community.* Ed. Lois Parkinson Zamora and Wendy B. Faris. Durham: Duke UP, 1995.

Smith, Michael Peter and Luis Eduardo Guarnizo. *Transnationalism from Below.* New Brunswick: Transaction Publishers, 1998.

Smith W. C. *Modern Islam in India.* Lahore: Iqbal Academy, 1947.

Spearey, Susan. "Shifting Continents/Colliding Cultures: Spatial Odysseys in Diaspora Writing." *Diaspora Writing of the Indian Subcontinent.* Ed. Ralph J. Crane and Radhika Mohanran. Atlanta: Rodopi B.V., 2000. 151–167.

Spivak, Gayatri Chakravorty. *Critique of Postcolonial Reason: Toward a History of the Vanishing Present.* Cambridge: Harvard UP, 1999.

———. *In Other Worlds: Essays in Cultural Politics.* New York: Routledge, 1988.

Suleri, Sara. "Contraband Histories: Salman Rushdie and the Embodiment of Blasphemy." *The Yale Review* 78.4 (1988): 62–78.

———. *Meatless Days.* Chicago: University of Chicago P, 1989.

Taylor, Charles. "The Politics of Recognition." *Multiculturalism: A Critical Reader.* Ed. David Theo Goldberg. Cambridge: Blackwell Publishers, 1994. 75–106.

Tiffin, Helen. "Commonwealth Literature and Comparative Methodology." *World Literature Written in English* 23:1 (1984).

Walsh, William. *Indian Literature in English.* London: Longman, 1990.

Waugh, Patricia. *Metafiction: The Theory and Practice of Self-Conscious Fiction.* New York: Metheun, 1984.

Weiss, Timothy F. *On the Margins: The Art of Exile in V.S. Naipaul.* Amherst: University of Massachusetts P, 1992.

Werbner, Pnina. "Introduction: the Dialectics of Cultural Hybridity." *Debating Cultural Hybridity: Multi-Cultural Identities and the Politics of Anti-Racism.* Ed. Pnina Werbner and Tariq Madood. London: Zed Books, 1997.

Williams, Raymond. *The English Novel: From Dickens to Lawrence.* Frogmore: Paladin, 1974.

Young, Robert J. C. *Postcolonialism: A Very Short Introduction.* New York: Oxford UP, 2003.

Index

Printed in the United States
100428LV00002B/27/A